Digital life story work

Using technology to help young people make sense of their experiences

Simon P Hammond and Neil J Cooper

Published by
CoramBAAF Adoption and Fostering Academy
41 Brunswick Square
London WC1N 1AZ
www.corambaaf.org.uk

Coram Academy Limited, registered as a company limited by guarantee
in England and Wales number 9697712, part of the Coram group, charity
number 312278

British Library Cataloguing in Publication Data
A catalogue record for this book is available from the British Library

ISBN 978 1 907585 67 8

Project management by Jo Francis, Publications Department, CoramBAAF
Designed and typeset by Helen Joubert Design
All photos posed by models, by www.istockphoto.com, and screengrabs
suppiled by the author
Printed in Great Britain by the Lavenham Press
Trade distribution by Turnaround Publisher Services, Unit 3, Olympia Trading
Estate, Coburg Road, London N22 6TZ

Contents

Acknowledgements

We would like to thank Norfolk County Council, BREAK and Hertfordshire County Council, their employees and the young people themselves. We would have no book without these people demonstrating the debt we owe. We also need to thank our colleagues Professor Gillian Schofield and Dr Beth Neil for their input and guidance at various stages during the four-year research project. We would like to thank Steve Gentry of Hertfordshire County Council for offering a practitioner perspective on the book, Andy Sayers and Jill Seeney for their reading of an early draft, and Shaila Shah and Jo Francis of BAAF for their assistance and support throughout.

Note about the authors

Dr Simon P Hammond recently completed his PhD upon which the majority of this book is based. He developed the idea of creating adolescent-specific digital life story work approaches in 2005 whilst working as a residential worker in Sheffield. Currently a Lecturer in Psychology at the University of East Anglia, Simon is extremely passionate about the everyday impact of research, committed to translating his research into practice and is an active contributor to the Centre for Research on Children and Families. He enjoys most things sporty, is known to tweet (@DrSiHammond) now and then and is a keen supporter of Nottingham Forest Football Club.

Dr Neil J Cooper is a Senior Lecturer in Psychology at the University of East Anglia. Neil's scholarly work orients around qualitative approaches in psychology and he has been involved in research concerning child protection, inter-professional practices, family support, and the use of technology in student learning and support. When not at work, Neil practices traditional karate, listens to Americana and walks up hills (although not usually at the same time).

Introduction

What is this book for?

When adolescents are supported and encouraged by caring adults, they thrive in unimaginable ways, becoming resourceful and contributing members of families and communities. Bursting with energy, curiosity and spirit that are not easily extinguished, young people have the potential to change negative societal patterns of behaviour and break cycles of violence and discrimination that pass from one generation to the next. With their creativity, energy and enthusiasm, young people can change the world in astonishing ways, making it a better place not only for themselves but for everyone.
(UNICEF, 2002, p. 3)

This book invites practitioners from all professions and carers who work with vulnerable adolescents to engage with them through digital life story work. Digital life story work involves using digital technologies to create opportunities for supportive conversations with young people which can help them to make sense of their past, their experiences and their aspirations.

This book builds on a four-year research project undertaken at the Centre for Research on Children and Families at the University of East Anglia, Norwich. The research project was Simon Hammond's PhD and was inspired by his time in practice as a residential worker.

During this time, Simon noticed that while some of the adolescents he worked with wanted to talk about their experiences, they were unwilling to engage using traditional life story work resources, frequently citing them as being "for kids". However, they would often use pictures and video clips on their mobile phones and talk to him about places and people from their past and present.

Informed by this, the original research project aimed to use the appeal of digital technology to develop adolescent-specific life story work resources. To do this, the project worked with young people, their carers and care providers to see if adolescent-specific resources would be used by the young people and how they would be received. Numerous interviews and focus groups with young people and carers were undertaken, and are drawn upon by this book to provide real-world quotes and case study examples.

The book is primarily for practitioners working with looked after young people, residential workers, foster carers and others, including adoptive parents. However, it is also relevant for therapists, counsellors and others who work with vulnerable young people. Building upon ideas about life story work, as an approach established in Ryan and Walker (first edition 1985 and updated many times, most recently in 2007), this book offers a range of illustrative, practical and jargon-free exercises which use technology to enable effective communication with adolescents.

Using this book

The book may be read from cover to cover, or dipped into according to your knowledge, confidence and needs.

- **Chapter 1, 'Why do digital life story work?'**, introduces the ideas behind digital life story work, outlining the importance of helping looked after young people reflect, with the aim of enhancing their self-understanding and sense of a coherent identity.

- **Chapter 2, 'Thinking about a project'**, introduces a number of creative individual "off the peg" ideas for digital life story projects. The level of technological skill needed across the nine projects ranges from beginner levels to those which intermediate computer users may find challenging at first.

- **Chapter 3, 'Working with young people'**, introduces ways to work with young people via technology.

- **Chapter 4, 'Preplanning, pitching and planning'**, looks at important aspects of planning a project and pitching it to the young person, to help ensure it will run smoothly.

- **Chapter 5, 'Creating content'**, looks at creating content, particularly filmed content, and points you may need to consider, including when filming in public.

- **Chapter 6, 'Editing and production'**, gives practical information on how to edit filmed content.

- **Chapter 7, 'Completing the project'**, gives some ideas for how to celebrate completing a project, including holding film premières.

- **Chapter 8, 'Towards tomorrow: storying the self'**, reinforces the ongoing need to discuss and listen to adolescents reflecting on their lives, highlighting how forthcoming innovations and research in the life story work field may present new ways to do this.

Finally, a series of appendices gives additional technological, practice and practical guidance, including details of equipment needed for digital life story work, a "jargon-buster", tips for filming and editing content, and resources which provide information on and can help to tackle cyberbullying.

Chapter 1
Why do digital life story work?

What is life story work and why is it important?

The ability to tell stories is a key part of everyday life. We are storytellers, with the most important story we have to tell often being about who we are. When we meet new people, we are normally called upon to tell this story. Commonly, these stories include information about where we were born, where we grew up, and so on. This knowledge tells others about who we are and informs our own self-understanding as we tell familiar stories and weave in new experiences. In childhood, in our everyday conversations with others and especially family members, information is given to us about how we fit into our family histories and carry on family characteristics. Children and young people who have had disruptive early life experiences may struggle to pull together information which enables them to create coherent life stories – that is, a story which they can easily understand. They may also have many significant questions about their early experiences to which they understandably want answers.

Life story work is often carried out with looked after children to fill in gaps in their self-knowledge and attempt to create a sense of coherence. The term is applied to a range of approaches commonly undertaken to aid the transition of younger children between short-term to long-term care and adoption placements. In this context, life story work seeks to help children to construct a story describing their own early life experiences and their relationships to those close to them. It is undertaken to assist children in establishing a keener understanding and acceptance of who they are, alongside how their past experiences have affected them.

Although there are a wide variety of approaches that fit under the umbrella term "life story work", there are some common underpinning ideas.

- Firstly, all the approaches seek to work with the child, their records and, where applicable, previous carers and birth family members to produce an age-appropriate explanation of how the child came into care and how they ended up living where they live today.

- Secondly, this work is undertaken so that the child may come to terms with, or at least be helped to manage, complex feelings towards birth relatives and previous carers.

- Thirdly, work is usually aimed at younger children up to the age of 12.

- Finally, each form of approach aims to create, with or for the child, a coherent biographical story.

Due to the emphasis on working with younger children, many life story work approaches use activities that younger children are comfortable with, proficient in and, in the case of different media, already using. For instance, younger children enjoy painting pictures and cutting out shapes; by using such activities adults facilitating life story work can record artwork and writing in life story work books, which provide a place for the carer and child to store and organise information. Although these books can be created for numerous reasons, including to provide a record of the work undertaken with the child, more importantly their production is an end goal of a therapeutic process. In this way, life story books are viewed as a product created as a consequence of the process of doing life story work. The book needs to be continually updated and can be used to construct answers to the growing child's questions about their past. The process of life story work includes discussions with and reflections by the child upon their story, supported by an adult in such a way that the child feels absolved of responsibility for their admission into care.

In the most recent edition of their book *Life Story Work* (2007), Tony Ryan and Rodger Walker sum up the benefits of undertaking life story work as a way of enabling troubled children to leave behind negative emotions that may have accumulated before and after moving into care. While life story work creates some form of resolution and aids transitions, when undertaken in childhood it needs to be continually revisited. From a psychological perspective, the benefits of being able to share one's stories, particularly those which contain emotional disclosures, have been shown to strengthen immune functioning, lower rates of depression and increase communication with others. Having one's story heard and understood by others can be a powerful and therapeutic experience; conversely, for those who do not feel their stories are heard or valued, this may lead to problems with emotional wellbeing and self-understanding, which in turn make for less than advantageous transitions to adulthood. Life story work can encourage reflection, aid self-knowledge development, identity coherence and sequential connections between important life events.

Despite the potential benefits of undertaking life story work with older looked after young people, it is generally thought of as something undertaken in childhood. The approaches used cater for younger children, which is not to say that older children do not enjoy activities such as making collages and drawing, but the resources which are produced to assist in life story work are designed to appeal to younger children and tend to be led by the professional.

Life story work with young people

This book acknowledges the benefits of undertaking life story work with younger children in care and seeks to widen the availability of these benefits to include adolescents. We start with the recognition that adolescents communicate in different ways than younger children and want to be treated and communicated with differently. The goal of widening access to the benefits of life story work through the promotion of its usage with adolescent care populations is informed by ideas derived from narrative psychology and the concept of communicative sensitivity – that is, making use of communication media commonly used by young people, and attending to the ways in which they use these media.

A narrative psychological approach emphasises humans as storytellers, and highlights how stories offer us an organising principle for experiences (since stories have a beginning, middle and end). This narrative understanding emphasises the importance of time when creating meaningful stories and how we use stories as a way to make sense of ourselves and others. The sharing and retelling of stories therefore becomes a way to enhance the understanding of important life events and their sequential relationship to each other. In this way, life story work is viewed as a way of facilitating the organisation of, and reflecting upon, lived experiences.

Communicative sensitivity emphasises the need to pay attention to how young people choose to communicate and encourages professionals to use similar methods. In the article 'Untold stories: a discussion of life story work' (Baynes, 2008), Polly Baynes focuses upon child-orientated approaches to life story work. In this discussion, she highlights the need for the adult working with a child to be 'prepared to make themselves vulnerable by entering the child's world and having the courtesy to communicate in the child's way' (p. 47). In this way, the importance of the communicative tools used during the life story work process double up as a way of conveying respect. This communicative sensitivity is perceived as a key element in the application of life story work to looked after adolescents. Adolescents have a stake in how their stories are told and a right to be listened to, and those working with young people need, as Baynes suggests, to enter the young person's world.

A window of opportunity

Adolescence is a term used to describe children aged 13–18 years of age. In the past, this phase of the life cycle has been linked with confrontation and seen as key in the formation of identity. Modern understandings view adolescence as a life phase that possesses a reflective quality, reinforcing the potential benefits of life story work to address self-knowledge gaps. The need to revisit life story work throughout adolescence has been highlighted but there is little in the way of detailed recommendations.

Adolescence offers an individual time to take stock before moving on to adult roles. This period of reflection can be considered to be especially important for adolescents living in care. They tend to have suffered more ambiguity in their lives, and therefore potentially have a great deal to reflect upon. In this way, adolescence can be seen as a window of opportunity for personal change, as opposed to a window that has already shut. This view invites the pursuit of new ways to communicate with vulnerable adolescents that may help them relate to others, manage their behaviour, understand their feelings and make beneficial decisions, helping them discover for themselves the value of making connections between past and present and articulate what is important to them in their life stories.

To capitalise upon this window of opportunity, attention needs to be paid to the way in which adolescents choose to communicate with those around them and each other. In acknowledging the use of digital technologies (including mobile phones, smartphones, digital cameras and camcorders, as well as laptops, desktop and tablet computers) by young people, the potential applications of these technologies to facilitate life story work emerges. Digital tools offer the ability to help young people to express thoughts and feelings which can be continually updated, edited and reflected upon. Using interactive computer-based media grants the user flexibility to make changes frequently and easily. Digital material can be copied, printed, saved or deleted as desired, making it an interesting medium for the construction of life story work. As well as the ability to continually make and remake digital creations, everyday technology represents a familiar, non-threatening, non-judgemental and non-invasive communication tool already used by many adolescents. Digital technologies can also record the more process-based elements of life story work, in that the relationship between the young person and the adult facilitating the work may be recorded. They enable young people to enjoy and reflect upon the reminders of the relationships and experiences, promoting reflection and reminiscence with those present at the time and also those new to viewing the material.

Adolescents, digital technologies and risk

For many people, digital technologies have become part of everyday life. In some cases technology is so commonplace that its importance is noticed only when it stops working. The use of digital technologies by adolescents is not without its potential problems, and these need to be explored before seeking to engage them. However, the potential harm of digital technologies is linked not to adolescents in particular, but rather to the growth of digital media in society in general.

Digital technologies are characterised here as the hardware or physical tools used to record text, images, sounds or both in the case of video clips. Computers, smartphones, cameraphones, digital cameras, camcorders and webcams are all examples of such technologies. Digital media tend to be intangible tools which allow users to connect with others and share created content. Social networking sites (SNS) such as Facebook, Bebo, Twitter, MySpace, Instant Messenger (IM), platforms such as MSN Chat, Skype, Facebook chat and Blackberry Messenger (BBM) as well as video and sharing websites/communities such as YouTube, Dailymotion and Blip.TV are all examples of digital media. Digital technologies and digital media are in many ways inextricably linked, as too are their potential benefits and risks. The most noticeable risks for those working with looked after children and young people include privacy, disclosure and cyberbullying.

Cyberbullying is a term used to describe a:

> ...child, preteen or teen being tormented, threatened, harassed, humiliated, embarrassed or otherwise targeted by another child, preteen or teen using the internet, digital technologies or mobile phones.
> (www.stopcyberbullying.org, accessed 6 June 2012)

This type of bullying can occur through a range of digital media including emails, in online chatrooms, instant messengers, text/picture/video messages sent to the victim's phone or posted on websites. When promoting the use of digital technologies and media, one needs to be aware of how to assist the young person in creating or using strategies to minimise the associated risks.[1]

For professionals working with looked after young people, the potential risks of digital technologies and media are of paramount importance, whether this involves looked after adolescents maintaining or getting in contact with those deemed inappropriate via social networking websites, or making deliberate/accidental disclosures in online domains due to an inability or a desire not to control privacy settings. Despite research in the US suggesting that public concerns regarding sexual predators using digital media may be exaggerated, the existence of paedophiles and the possibilities of online grooming reinforce the need to manage risk, particularly as real world vulnerabilities tend to be replicated online.[2] It is worth noting, however, that research appears to emphasise how social networking websites are mainly used as an economic way to maintain pre-existing offline friendships;[3] Lenhart and Madden (2007) report that the vast majority of their US adolescent sample used social networking websites to connect or reconnect with previously known friends. Such potential benefits may be particularly important to looked after populations as adolescents in care have consistently reported feelings of social and geographical isolation, a point stressed by Professor Andrew Kendrick in his contribution to *Facing Forward: Residential child care in the 21st century* (2005). We need to be aware that although looked after young people may be locally isolated, digital technologies enable them to be remotely connected. These advantages need to be viewed in relation to the young person in question and what such contact may mean to them.

---

1 A range of websites and web resources have been created to combat cyberbullying; see Appendix 3.

2 For more practical advice on the use of SNS by looked after populations, see the excellent and comprehensive book *Social Networking and Contact* (Fursland, 2010).

3 See 'Facebook friend or Facebook foe?' (Hammond, 2011), for an accessible insight into this area.

The internet and digital technologies are like cars, in that they are not dangerous in themselves, but in how they can be used. How technology is used by young people and those who wish to take advantage of vulnerable populations is where dangers and risks should be located. We need to help young people to learn to drive safely on their own, and negotiate an increasingly complex online and digital world. By engaging with digital life story work, young people can receive a wide array of benefits, as the workers or carers undertaking the work can use this opportunity to engage with the young people in a communicatively sensitive fashion, allowing for conversations regarding the wider uses and risks of such technologies, promoting technological responsibility and safety.

Digital technologies in life story work

Digital technologies and their relevant software offer unprecedented flexibility to create and edit audio, audiovisual and photographic material. The high value placed on digital technologies by adolescents means that just the very use of computers can attract the attention of disengaged and socially excluded young people. Digital technologies and media, such as the mobile phone and internet, provide an attractive approach to use with this group, as it conforms with their existing practice of using such technology to spontaneously record events from their worlds.

In seeking to make the benefits of life story work available to adolescent care populations through digital technologies, we should realise that simply integrating technology into existing life story work approaches is unlikely to engage adolescents. Additionally, the more adult-led approaches to life story work, which have clear benefits when working with younger children, may need to be altered when working with young people. Digital life story work seeks to be less prescriptive and more participatory than conventional work undertaken with younger children. Nevertheless, there is still the fundamental need to familiarise oneself with records that provide information about the young person's life and reasons for coming into care and to assess the risks of digital life story work with the individual.

Digital life story work aims to support adolescents in the production of, and reflections upon, the stories they choose to share. However, the introduction and inclusion of digital communication tools does not detract from the central role played by the relationship created during this process. Though the communication media used to facilitate this relationship and portray the young people's stories are different from traditional life story work, the importance of an engaged, sensitive and caring adult, carer or professional is not.

Adolescents will only share stories if there is an audience to share them with. This audience plays a pivotal role in the construction and production of, and reflections upon, these stories. As storytellers, we may tell the same story differently depending upon this audience. The role of the adult who facilitates digital life story work is complex and discussed in more detail in Chapter 3. For now, it is sufficient to highlight that this adult needs to balance the participatory ethos of digital life story work alongside negotiating the responsible and safe use of digital technologies, whilst also supporting young people's reflections on what could be a host of fragmented and emotionally sensitive memories.

Technological difficulties

Show me a person who never made a mistake and I will show you a person who never achieved anything.

Regardless of one's level of proficiency, or indeed the proficiency level of the adolescent you aim to undertake digital life story work with, you should recognise that occasionally technological difficulties will arise. A point worth remembering is that the digital equipment referred to throughout this book is simply a tool that can fill a range of needs. It is how these tools are used in the relationship experienced between the adolescent and adult that is the key factor.

When working with digital technologies, there are certain points to keep in mind. You will need to be patient and remain optimistic – try to use any technological problems as opportunities for engagement with the young person. Suggest resolutions and ways in which problems can be managed together – listen to the young person, as their suggestions may resolve the problem. Above all, you will need to have a sense of humour and the ability to learn from mistakes. We all get frustrated with technology but it is important not to get overly frustrated with the technology in front of the young person. This may be an obvious point to make but it is worth emphasising – if the young person decides to take their frustrations out on the digital technology, this may be a costly lesson to learn.

In an attempt to avoid unnecessary and potentially costly frustrations, it is a good idea to "play" with the hardware (the technology itself) and software (the programmes which run the hardware) yourself before attempting to engage the young person. Try one or two of the projects in Chapter 2 for yourself from start to finish; this will give you an insight into how the equipment can be used and a firsthand experience of the processes involved from a young person's perspective. Doing this will also enable you to ensure that, when it comes to later stages such as editing and production, the software you need is already installed and both you and the young person are fairly familiar with how it works (more advice about installing software and hardware is provided in Chapter 6). On a final note, it may be worth investing in "whatever happens" or accidental damage insurance, or checking whether this is covered under your household or workplace insurance (where applicable) and if this insurance stretches to accidental damage outside the home or office. Accidents happen and accidents with electrical equipment can be costly.

Chapter 2
The projects

Thinking about a project

This chapter provides some ideas for digital life story work projects which can be started and completed in short time frames. Because those reading this book and looking to undertake digital life story work will have different levels of technological knowledge, the chapter is not designed to take you step-by-step through every potential decision involving technology. Instead, the chapter encourages you to work together with young people to explore and exploit the possibilities of digital media. By working on small projects, you will build up skills and ways of working in partnership that you can expand upon as you develop and undertake ongoing work. The book, and especially this chapter, provides starting points from which you can begin to build up ideas for your own projects.[1]

When starting any of the projects introduced in this chapter, one of the best ways to learn about the process is by doing it from start to finish and learning from mistakes.

How to use the projects

The projects are not listed to work through in order; any project can be used as a starting point depending on the young person you are working with, your interest, resources and what life story materials you have available or want to create. Having a few different projects to consider helps you to negotiate what sort of activities are possible and what would be interesting for any individual young person. As some people may be less assured than others with the use of computers, the types of activity suggested are relatively simple so you do not have to get too bogged down with the technology. It is important to keep in mind that the technology is a tool for engaging young people. As your working relationship grows stronger and confidence builds, you will want to explore more

1 See the appendices for additional technological guidance if appropriate.

challenging and sensitive issues in relation to the young person's experience and emotions. The technology will gradually become less important and the process of dealing with feelings and putting events into perspective will become more prominent.

Digital technology is part of the everyday world of young people. Websites such as Facebook, Twitter and YouTube have come to occupy a central role in many adolescents' lives, as has communicating through instant messaging and Skype. While the products of the projects suggested in this chapter all have the potential to be linked with internet activity, the decision to place any material onto public internet spaces needs careful consideration and discussion (see Chapter 3 for a more in-depth discussion about this). Your workplace may also specify guidelines and local policy which should direct and inform any decisions about the public sharing of material, and these guidelines should be checked at an early stage. As the activities are creative and fun, some projects which can be separated off from the digital life story work could be made available to a wider audience. Indeed, working with young people around these issues can help to open up discussions about the appropriate negotiation of personal and digital boundaries.

Tip

Before you start to create any digital material, it is a good idea to think about how you are going to save it. If you have easy access to a computer you may like to create a folder where all digital material and projects can be saved. If appropriate, ensure that this is undertaken in accordance with organisational policy.

Also think about backing up this material either to a storage device like a USB drive or DVD. As you work with a young person, you may develop digital material of a personal and sensitive nature, so ways of maintaining privacy such as password-protected computers and profiles also need to be considered at this stage.

We have suggested nine initial projects.

Project	In a nutshell	Time required
1. Remaking memories	Digitising old photos or images.	2–3 hours
2. Digital audio stories	Recording a personal story and saving as an audio file (typically an mp3).	3–4 hours
3. Points of view	Interviewing or being interviewed – either on video or audio.	3–4 hours
4. Soundscape	Creating an audio representation of either everyday background sounds or sounds of a specific location or event.	Any short time period for recording
5. Life tracks	Linking music with emotions and meanings.	2–3 hours
6. Photo mashup	Making a photo collage using online tools.	1–4 hours

Project	In a nutshell	Time required
7. Toontime	Making a comic strip about a real or imagined experience.	2 hours
8. Three-minute movie	Making a three-minute movie.	3–4 hours
9. Podwalk	Revisiting significant locations with a video camera and recording stories the places evoke, then burning these to DVD to be watched with the young person.	Minimum of a day

Tip

Because all the projects involve the use of digital technology, they are fairly easy to integrate, re-edit and re-use. This means that content you have created, such as digital pictures, audio recordings or video clips, can be combined or linked with other projects; over time, ongoing projects can build and develop substantial pieces of work.

Project 1: Remaking memories
(2–3 HOURS)

One aspect of life story work is looking back at past events, thinking and talking about important people and reflecting upon how situations or relationships may have changed. One way to look backwards is to use old photographs in a way in which they can be gathered together, reviewed and talked about. While digital photos are very common today, some photos of significant people or places may exist only as old prints. Digitising old photos can be an easy and fun process, and the visual images provide a background for discussion and reflection. Because some photos may evoke overwhelming emotions which can lead to young people destroying them and then almost instantly regretting doing so, digitising old photos can help to keep a safe and permanent record.

If you have do not have access to technology such as a scanner, you can digitise photos at many high street photographic stores that often offer a digitising service. This is a more expensive method of digitising photos, and an opportunity of discussing them with the young person involved will be lost, but this can be recaptured when editing and embellishing the images.

If young people have no old photos, you can use more recent images taken with a digital camera, cameraphone or smartphone, and use this opportunity to enhance them and store them in an organised way. Thinking about a simple theme such as "friends" can be useful for guiding you about what photos to take or use.

What you need

A small number of old photos

A means of copying the photos onto a computer (a scanner or even a camera or cameraphone)

A computer with photo editing software (such as Photoshop) or access to the internet

A printer (if printing out the edited photos)

What you do

- **Choosing photos:** Pick a few photos to digitise (four or five is probably enough). If you use too many, the process can become a bit repetitive.

- **Scanning:** Scan each photo.

- **Editing:** Edit, enhance and save each photo.

- **Taking breaks:** If you are working with a young person who finds it difficult to concentrate for a long period, it may be useful to break up the session – you could work with them in selecting the photos and then scan the images in yourself before working together on the editing.

Instructions

Below, the basic scanning process is explained. There are many different scanners and combined printer-scanners on the market, and specific instructions may vary depending on the make and model.

1. Make sure the scanner is linked to the computer. When you turn the scanner on, this often opens up the correct software on the computer. If not, click on the software icon from the start menu.

2. Put your photo onto the glass scanner surface with the image face down, placing it tight into the corner. You may need to clean the glass first so there are no smudges which might affect the image.

3. Many scanners automatically set the DPI (scanner resolution). If you want to set this manually, 300 DPI should be sufficient.

4. Scan the photo by either clicking SCAN on the software or pressing the scan button on the scanner. It is usually possible to preview what you have scanned, which makes it easy to spot odd mistakes, although remember that many image issues can be resolved with editing software.

5. Once the image is scanned, your software will usually prompt you to save the image. Find the folder you have identified for saving material, or find the MY PICTURES folder. Save the image as a .jpeg (some scanners may automatically do this).

Tip

When scanning, if you use a high resolution setting this may mean your photos require a large memory storage space. Resolution is measured by DPI (dots per inch); 300 DPI is fine for most photos.

Now you have a digital photo, you can edit it using editing software. There are many different editing packages available, but all allow you to crop/resize and generally improve the photo. In many photo editing programmes, text can be added, enabling the young person to name people in a photo or comment about the story the photo represents. Many programmes allow you to choose different frames for your image and this can add more fun to the process. Do not worry too much about the final outcome of the editing, especially if you are new to using photo editing software; the key thing is to enjoy the process and to get the young person to talk about the photos. Any mistakes can easily be undone on most packages.

Tip

Make a copy of your photo before you start editing, so if anything does go wrong, you can always start again with the copy.

6. Open your photo editing software and open your copied photo. You may see something similar to Figure 1 (see below).

7. Crop the photo if necessary; this usually involves clicking on an item such as EDIT in the tool bar. Typically, you will be presented with a box or corners which you can move with the mouse to create the size of photo you want. This allows you to crop unwanted sections of photos such as too much sky, so the focus is on the person or place of interest.

Figure 1: Screenshot showing editing tool bar and cropping tool in action, with shaded area of the image being the area to be cropped

8. Red-eye removal: in many old photos, people have red eyes caused by the flash of the camera. Photo editing software, such as that used in Figure 1, can usually get rid of this by colouring in the redness.

9. Enhance the sharpness of the image and adjust the lighting to avoid dark or light areas.

10. Fun embellishing can be done with some programmes which allow you to place frames around the photo or add artistic effects – try a few out.

Once you have a good quality photo, there are some online sites which allow you to add lots of great effects to create works of art. One site is www.befunky.com, which is simple to use and can quickly produce a stunning effect, as shown in Figure 2.

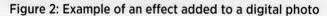

Figure 2: Example of an effect added to a digital photo

Result

Now you have your digital images, you can go on to create more, or you can consider presenting the photos in different ways. Do you want to produce new enhanced prints from the old photos? Do you want to store and view the photos in a digital photo frame or on a computer? Many high street photographic stores and websites also provide services to print photos onto mugs, keyrings and other items, which can create a constant reminder of a significant place or person.

A simple way of presenting the images on your computer is to use them to create a desktop background (the background image which is on the screen when you start up the computer). Instructions to do this are given below.

1. From your documents folder, navigate to your image files.

2. Right click on the image you want to use. A box will appear with options – one of which is SET AS DESKTOP BACKGROUND or some similar phrase. Left click this option and your picture will automatically appear on the start-up screen (see Figure 3).

3. There are many shortcut ways of presenting several images in a changing slideshow. Instructions vary depending on what system you are using, but if you click the start menu and then the control panel, there will be an option

for creating a slide show on the desktop, sometimes under a term such as PERSONALISE.

Figure 3: Screenshot of setting a picture as a desktop background

Take care

There are many photo-sharing websites, such as Flickr, and social media websites like Facebook, which make posting digital pictures online very easy. It is also easy to share images by email. Posting or sharing any image needs careful consideration and should be undertaken in line with the organisational policy of your workplace, where appropriate.

Digital life story work elements

- **Acknowledging and listening to emotions:** Looking at photos is often a spontaneous shared activity as people and situations are identified and described. While looking at photos, many questions may come to mind: Who is in the photo? Who is absent? What's the tale behind the photo? In this shared experience small stories are captured, which can be revisited and revised as further projects are undertaken. Talking about people and places from the past raises emotions and these need to be acknowledged and explored over time. When you first try this sort of project with a young person, you may become focused on the technology, but as you become familiar with the tools, make time to look at the photos and talk about their content. Encourage the young person to take more digital photos and save them as they can be worked with in the future.

- **Connotations of cropping photos:** The advantage of being able to digitally crop an image is that, unlike conventional photos, the user can press UNDO or revert to the original copy – as long as the image is backed up. However, when cropping people from photos, it is important to remember that simply cropping a photo does not remove the individual from the young person's biography; instead, it allows the young person to place an individual present in the photo in a psychological position within a story acceptable to them at a point in time. This will be discussed in Chapter 6, but highlighting it here demonstrates how editing content can impact upon how stories can be told and retold.

Extending the project

Try embedding the photos in a film by joining them together with an audio commentary (see later projects in this chapter for instructions). You can record the young person talking about the photo and the story behind it, and link the commentary with a photo slideshow.

Project 2: Digital audio stories
(3–4 HOURS)

This project makes use of whatever recording technology you have available (mobile phones, webcams, etc) to recount a short story from the young person's life. You can build on and combine techniques from the other projects in this chapter to add images to illustrate the story if you have time, perhaps getting the young person to record their memories from older photos used in the Remaking memories project.

Tip

Before recording the story, think about who it is for. What do you want to say? It may take a while to think about the "right" idea to use, and a story which has a clearly defined beginning, middle and end will work best. Having a particular audience in mind will help young people get the tone right.

Most computers will come with a pre-installed audio editor as part of video editing software; Windows Movie Maker (for PCs) and iMovie (for Mac) can also be used to edit audio files. Failing this, there are many free audio editors available to download from the internet, for example, Audacity, shown in Figure 4 (http://audacity.sourceforge.net).

Figure 4: Screenshot showing how an audio file appears in Audacity

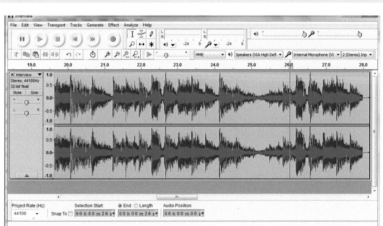

If you are working with a young person who is still mastering English, try using Google Translate (http://translate.google.com) to help out. This is an easy package to use, in which you can type in sentences in many different languages and get instant translations.

What you need

A computer/laptop

Audio recording equipment (such as a mobile phone or laptop). A desktop PC can also be used to record audio files, but this is best undertaken with a headphone set with an attached microphone.

Audio editing software

What you do

- **Pick a story:** Decide on the story you want to tell.

- **Find a quiet area:** Make sure you have enough time to record the story.

- **Mistakes?** Do not worry about making mistakes when recording – just keep on talking, as you can edit out mistakes and restarts after you have finished recording.

- **Editing:** Edit the tale using audio editing software.

- **Saving:** Save the tale as an mp3 file so it can be listened to on many different devices.

Tip

Finding a truly quiet place is important. Even a place we think of as quiet can actually include background noise levels which can be picked up by a digital recorder. Background noise is difficult to edit out and is best avoided. More importantly, if a young person is retelling a sensitive story, privacy is very important.

Instructions

1. Practise with the device you are going to use. Many laptops have inbuilt webcams which young people may wish to use to record their story.

2. When you are ready, press RECORD and start the story.

3. Once you have finished telling the story, press STOP.

4. If you are recording directly onto a computer or laptop, most software packages will automatically save your recordings to a default file. If you are recording on a device such as a mobile phone, after recording you will have to

connect the phone to the computer, identify the sound file and copy it to your designated folder.

5. Open the sound file in your audio software package. Your recording will appear as a long series of waves. If you press PLAY, a line will move along the wave and you can identify where any editing is needed.

6. Edit out any verbal mistakes so the story flows smoothly. This can be done by highlighting the section of the wave which contains the problem area and clicking CUT or pressing the delete key.

7. If you click SAVE, many packages will save your work as an editing project, which can take up a lot of memory. Instead, when you have done some editing, save the edited version as an mp3 file; this is often done by "exporting" the file rather than saving it. To do this, click EXPORT AS MP3 and give the file a new name.

8. Continue to edit as you want. Consider using other editing tools, such as amplifying areas of the recording which are too quiet.

9. When you are happy with the edited version, save it as an mp3 file. If you have an audience in mind, store the file and play it for them when convenient.

Result

Saving a story as an mp3 audio file means it can be shared with others very easily; it can also be played in the absence of the young person, and can even be sent by email. This means that a young person can take time to retell a story until they are happy with it before they either keep it for themselves or share it with other appropriate people.

Take care

Stories can include details of a personal nature. Like digital photos, the sharing benefits of digital audio files have potential negative aspects and care needs to be taken about who should hear the digital stories and how the material is stored. Again, refer to the organisational policy of your workplace and take reasonable steps to ensure confidentiality is maintained, where appropriate.

Tip

Encouraging young people to talk about and record their feelings can also be used to help them to have their voices heard in various review meetings, which many young people can find intimidating or frustrating to attend.

Digital life story work elements

- Using technology to tell a story is still telling a story, and it involves all the usual tools of storytelling, such as characters, plot and emotions. It may be useful to go over the story a few times, thinking about how characters are represented and how emotions are expressed. It is best if the story has some important meaning for the young person, or is a story which the young person wants to tell to someone. You might start with a simple story and gradually develop the retelling of more significant experiences as you become comfortable with the technology.

  Many young people who have had difficult early experiences have a stock of stories which they are used to telling to professionals and others; starting with an accessible story such as this and then prompting the young person for more information can help to ensure that details which tend to be glossed over are included.

- Many young people will have experienced multiple moves and changes of carer. This story technique offers a way to complete episodes and create endings which may have been missed. The ability to edit the story may become more useful as stories are developed and young people recall a missing element or link which can be recorded at a later date and inserted so the story builds in completeness over time.

Extending the project

The story can be used as a soundtrack for a short film, or music can be added to the beginning and end. If a series of stories is created, placing these in an appropriate order may provide a sense of the changes and stabilising elements in the young person's life, and emphasise relationships between sequences of important life events.

Having a series of stories that reflect upon more recent events, such as leaving a school, can also help the young person to direct their thoughts to the future. Discussing aspirations can help young people to think more positively about their futures and allow you to introduce notions of changing elements of their current lives to help this imagined future become a reality.

Audio letters or stories to projected future selves at landmark ages such as 16, 18 and 21 can be helpful for young people. These can provide an opportunity for you to help the young person think about their current behaviours and the impact of these both in the present and on their future self and aspirations.

Ask the young person if they want their digital audio stories burnt to a CD to keep them safe. Ask if a copy can be kept with their care records in case their copy gets scratched, lost or broken.

Project 3: Points of view
(3–4 HOURS)

This project sets up a few simple interviews, with two formats to choose from.

- The young person can take the lead as interviewer, allowing them to control the action, ask the questions and edit the final content.

- The young person could also choose to be interviewed, placing them at the centre of the action.

Interviewing others gives you the opportunity to talk to the young person about how questions are asked and how to follow up issues. This project will work best if you concentrate on a specific issue or topic that people have different views about and an area which interests the young person. The topic could be something simple and domestic, such as whether the car needs cleaning or the garden needs tidying, or more opinionated and political, such as access issues for wheelchair users or animal rights, or something more applicable to the young person's situation, such as how to welcome fostered children into a new home.

What you need

Audio recording equipment, such as a mobile phone or laptop/computer with a microphone (or webcam). Video equipment can also be used.

A computer with audio editing software (see Digital audio stories project above).

What you do

- **If you are going to interview using audio:** Listen to an interview or two on the radio. Check how the interviewer introduces the conversation, focuses on a couple of points, and thanks the interviewee.

- **If you are going to interview using video:** Look at how interviewees on TV are framed and how camera angles are used.

- **If the young person is going to interview people:** Decide on who would be good to interview and what sorts of things to ask. Make sure the person whom you plan to interview is happy to be recorded and is aware of how the recording may be used.

- **Work with the young person to develop a range of questions:** These need to be suitable to ask other people, or that the young person wants an interviewer to ask them. Go over what sort of questions would be best to ask and to avoid.

- **Think about the interview style you want to adopt:** If it will be a formal interview, plan a few questions to ask; if it will be more casual, think about where and when people would be available to talk (remember to identify a quiet place).

- **Pick a specific theme or issue to talk about:** Encourage the young person to formulate questions which encourage people to speak; for example, it is more interesting to ask, 'Tell us about your favourite food', rather than 'What is your favourite food?'

- **Staging an interview:** The interview does not need to be staged; it can be recorded as people are doing other tasks, as long as it does not interfere with an activity.

- **Plan any introductions and conclusions that might be needed:** If you do not want to undertake too much editing, record the introduction, then undertake the interviews, and then record the conclusion.

Tip

When interviewing, leaving the recorder running means you will have a long sound file, but this can be edited into shortened chunks and ensures that you capture people talking and do not miss interesting comments.

Instructions

1. Practise using the equipment.

2. If you are using a device such as a mobile phone, make sure you can start and stop a recording and that the device has enough memory to take a recording which may last 10 minutes. It is also a good idea to practise copying a file onto the computer before you start interviewing.

3. Although an interview can be carried out in busy places, it is surprising how much background noise can be picked up by a microphone. Choose a fairly quiet place to talk.

4. Remember to press PLAY! Start the interview by introducing the person, ask questions, and close by thanking them. Remember to press STOP!

5. If using a mobile device, once the interview is finished, connect the device to the computer and copy the sound file into the designated folder. If you are using a laptop or PC, when you stop recording the software will usually prompt you to save the file; name it in a memorable way.

Now for the editing bit.

6. There are many audio editing packages. If you have made a recording with a computer, the recording software will probably include editing options.

7. If you are new to editing, the software can look a bit complex at first as it displays the sound in a wave format. By pressing play you will usually see the

progress of the sound along the wave and can click on the wave at any point and drag the mouse to indicate which bits of sound you want to edit.

8. If you are unsure, try a few simple techniques like deleting some of the recording. If there is background noise between questions, you can insert a short period of silence to block this out.

9. If some interviewees have louder voices than others, select segments of the wave which carry the quieter voices and amplify these.

10. When you are happy with the editing, save the file as an mp3.

Result

You should aim to produce an mp3 file with a short (3–5 minute) piece of audio which carries a few points on the topic in question.

Take care

Conversation that you have recorded can be reworked and re-used. Make sure that any manipulation of people's voices is not used in embarrassing contexts, and if the interview is going to be used beyond what was originally agreed (such as added to a film soundtrack), make sure the interviewee is happy with this. Young people may choose to interview each other; in this case, it is important to consider the issues to be discussed and to agree which issues should not be talked about.

Digital life story work elements

- By interviewing people, we are getting them to talk about their own experiences, which may seem counter to life story work agendas, which usually focus on the young person. However, thinking about other people's perspectives and including others' voices helps to explore the wider connections of a young person's life. This project will bring up issues involved in the digital life story work process, as it offers an opportunity for young people to talk "on tape" and to think about what questions are appropriate to ask, who should ask them, and how best to frame them if they wish to talk to important people from their pasts. Young people can think about the way in which they communicate with others and how to represent their own and others' views.

- By experiencing being interviewed, the young person can practise presenting a particular impression, and talk about things they are knowledgeable about or have strong views about, which can boost self-confidence.

- The less sensitive applications of this project, such as creating a short news piece about whether or not the car needs cleaning, can also begin to build up digital skills for a later stage when more emotive subjects are approached.

Extending the project

By collecting together a number of short interviews, a perspective on an issue of shared experiences can be built up. As skills develop, it may be possible to interview people from the young person's past and present. This will take longer to arrange and may need to be carefully considered, but can help to make connections between the young person's past, present and future.

Project 4: Soundscape
(ANY SHORT TIME PERIOD)

A soundscape is a particular sound or combination of sounds which represent everyday acoustic environments. By using an audio recording device, the soundscape project invites young people to record the sounds which make up their world. This project explores the current situation of the young person, although it can be used to go back to a place and build up a soundscape of a specific location or short journey. This could be planned and have a theme (perhaps "a day in the life") where specific sounds are sought in a planned way, beginning with an alarm clock, for example. This project may be especially useful for a young person with vision impairment, inviting others to share the young person's experiences of their world.

If sounds from a particular location cannot be obtained, the young person may want to construct an imaginary soundscape or journey by using sound files which are freely available on the internet through sites such as http://commons.wikimedia.org. Some websites that have many free sounds, such as www.freesound.org, may require you to register before you can download sounds.

What you need

Audio recording equipment (mobile phone, laptop)

A computer with audio editing software

Internet access (if using free sound effects websites)

What you do

- **Decide on the timeframe:** How long do you want to record for? What kinds of sounds which might make up the soundscape?

- **Is the soundscape about a specific location?** If yes, plan what sort of sounds represent the place and think about how to order them so they can provide reference points to the place.

Tip

If you are including people's conversations, make sure they are aware that you are recording them.

To reduce editing, it can be helpful to record sounds in the order in which you want to present them.

Instructions

1. Check the equipment and batteries.

2. It might be useful to get the young person to describe what they are doing or what the next sound is, especially when recording a few sounds that are similar.

3. When all sounds have been recorded, transfer them onto your computer.

4. Open the editing software and open a new track. As you open or import each sound, add it to your developing soundscape.

5. Editing for this project might be challenging, as the different sounds may need amplifying or quietening to fit with the overall balanced effect. Check out the editing possibilities, which are usually found under a tab labelled EFFECT.

6. It is also possible to fade in and fade out sounds in many editing packages. This means that some sounds can be slowly brought into the soundscape or grow fainter to avoid sudden mood changes.

7. Save the completed soundtrack as an mp3 file.

Result

The young person will have created an mp3 file designed to transport listeners to the place or time of the sounds by evoking the atmosphere of the environment.

Digital life story work element

The background sounds to everyday life often go unnoticed. Sounds from the environment can help to connect to memories, and hearing a specific sound can prompt a memory. Listening to a soundscape can also produce thoughts about how an environment or living situation has changed, as well as what is absent. If you are working with young people who have lived in other cultures or particular environments, for instance, in an inner city, or by the sea, what they pick out as important sounds can be surprising. When developing a soundscape about the past, going to locations to collect sounds with young people may not be possible but having someone collect sounds for them is more manageable, and they can then edit and develop the audio. How the sounds link to places and people can be talked through during the editing process.

Extending the project

In capturing sounds from everyday life, a sound archive is also created which can be combined with other projects. Adding sounds that remind the young person of a picture created in the Remaking memories project, for example, could see a picture of a person or place displayed alongside the sounds from the place.

Project 5: Life tracks
(2–3 HOURS)

Having a music collection and listening to music is an important part of many young people's lives. This project aims to link music to feeling and events; it revolves around music and encourages young people to join together or link a number of pieces of music with talk in between tracks.

Warning – copyright issues!

At present, you cannot copy CDs and mp3 files which you have purchased, as it is illegal under UK law (for further details see the Intellectual Property Office: www.ipo.gov.uk). There is a proposal to change copyright law to enable copying for private use. Some "royalty free" music is available online, although this is not always free of charge. There are some interesting sites which offer a selection of music which can be copied and re-edited under a creative commons licence (see http://creativecommons.org/licenses/ for further information).

The website http://opsound.org/ offers a wide variety of musical genres and artists which are free to copy and edit. Some sites, such as www.openmusicarchive.org/, provide mp3 music where the UK copyright has expired. These are often very old recordings, but can be fun to use. The website http://incompetech.com/m/c/royalty-free/ has a wide variety of interesting files, including music used for silent films, African drumming and much more.

This book assumes that when the term "track" is used, it is acknowledged that the authors are not promoting the use of illegally obtained or copied music.

What you need

A computer with internet access

A digital audio recording device – many mobile phones and laptops have this facility

Audio editing software

What you do

- **Choosing:** Choose an episode or event to link with music.

- **How long a time period?** You can choose to look back over a lengthy period such as the last school year, but this might be very time consuming, so it is best to consider a short period which involves a specific mood. This could be something simple such as first impressions of a new place, or exploring a behaviour or feeling.

- **Finding music:** Access a free music website such as those suggested above.

- **Discuss:** Set out the background circumstances of the event with the young person by talking through what happened.

- **Selecting tracks:** When the young person starts to recount a feeling, check through the different types of music and select a particular track which reflects the mood.

- **Associations:** Sounds could also be associated with specific characters or places.

By switching between available music and reflecting upon events, the young person can reach a point where they want to describe a feeling and insert a sound to convey the feeling.

Instructions

1. Record the introduction setting the scene to the life track using your audio recording device (mobile phone, laptop, etc).

2. Identify a feeling, place or person and select the music which best fits the feeling.

3. Open your audio editing software and open or import the spoken introduction.

4. Identify, select and copy the music you want to keep. Edit and paste the music you have selected into your introduction. You can fade in and fade out the music on most audio editing packages.

5. Continue the spoken introduction until the next sound is required and again find and insert the sound or music which best fits the description.

6. Gradually fill out the episode or event with the music or sounds and end with a sound or music which finishes off the track and sums up the end feeling.

7. Save the edited file as an mp3 file.

Result

The young person will produce an outline story of an event or episode mixed with music or sounds which convey the different moods in the story to the listener. This can produce a dramatic effect.

Digital life story work element

Music is great for tapping into our emotions, likes and dislikes, and can often form the backdrop to significant times in our lives. Young people frequently enjoy music, and talking about why they like a particular track or artist and what it means to them can open up a way of discussing feelings.

Extending the project

Linking music to an event opens up a way of talking about feelings. Consider linking these events and their feelings into some form of meaningful order.

Project 6: Photo mashup
(1–4 HOURS)

This project can build on previous photographic projects or be completely new. It involves taking or obtaining a number of images and arranging them together so they express a relationship. The photos could be selected to portray any connection, including people, places, or the young person themselves in different poses or at different ages.

Some websites allow you to upload photos and create collages in different shapes for saving on the computer or home printing. Websites such as http://fotonea.com are easy to use and can create collages for free (although some sites limit the number of images you can use). An interesting artistic feel can be created through http://bighugelabs.com/hockney.php. This website can produce a great effect by using one image which the website reproduces and arranges as a number of overlapping images. Collages can also be created in many photo editing software packages. There are also a range of collage making "apps" (downloadable programmes) available for mobile phones and smartphones.

What you need

A computer with internet access

Old photos which are in digital format (see Project 1)

OR Time to take new photos around a specific theme

What you do

Either select old photos and digitise them (see Project 1) or select recent digital photos. If you are going to use recent photos, set aside some time to take specific shots, for example, encourage the young person to take photos of a number of friends, areas of their house, etc.

Tip

While you can mix and match photos in a creative way, for your first attempts it may be best to use photos which have similar dimensions and similar sized contents. You can edit the photos first to make sure the contents, such as faces, are roughly the same size. If you are including people's conversations, make sure they are aware that you are recording them.

Instructions

1. Scan your photo, take your new photos or download your images. Save them as .jpeg files in your designated folder.

2. Access the internet and select the collage website you want to use.

3. Some websites provide you with a downloadable programme. If you choose to download a programme, make sure you have permission to save this onto the computer and that you have up-to-date antivirus software.

4. If using a website, it will usually prompt you to upload photos. If you are doing a collage of one picture, you will just need to upload one photo. If you are using several photos, repeat the uploading process for all the photos you want to have in the collage.

5. Some websites provide further options such as the space of your collage, or a frame style or background.

6. The website will then prompt you to save your collage. Save it with a name which makes sense and in a location that can be easily found.

7. If you have colour printing facilities you could print out the collage; if not, some high-street photographic stores may be able to do this.

Result

You will have a collage of photos which work around a theme; this can be printed out, displayed on your computer or printed at most high-street photographic stores. It may be worth ensuring there is a backup copy kept somewhere safe in case of damage.

Digital life story work element

It is important to remember that the key elements of this project are the conversations with the young person about the people, places and relationships in the photos. Arranging the photos in a way that is visually appealing will involve discussing the interconnections between the images.

Extending the project

As with more traditional collages, there are countless numbers of possible themes which photo mashups can take. For young people struggling to make sense of complex family situations or living arrangements, for example, a new foster family, families from differing cultural backgrounds or many half- or step-siblings, photo mashups may provide a way for young people to talk about such circumstances and their feelings about them.

Project 7: Toontime
(2 HOURS)

This project uses websites to create a comic strip of a real or imagined event or experience. You can also create simple comic strips with your own photos in a word processing file. There are many websites which allow you to make characters and write dialogue. Sometimes this is a bit fiddly and you may need a little time to practise. Some websites, such as www.pixton.com, www.stripcreator. com and www.bitstrips.com/, require you to register an account if you wish to save your comic strip.

Website such as www.makebeliefscomix.com have a standard range of characters but you can introduce your own dialogue (see Figures 5 and 6).

Figure 5: Screenshot from www.makebeliefscomix.com

Figure 6: A screenshot taken from www.makebeliefscomix.com

What you need

A computer with internet access

Some photos or images

What you do

1. A really simple way to extend the project and make use of digital photos is to insert photos and speech bubbles in a Word document.

2. Open a new Word document.

3. It is best to use a landscape page layout, rather than portrait, as this will give you more room for the images. Click FILE then PAGE SETUP, PAPER SIZE, and finally click the LANDSCAPE option.

4. Keep things simple by creating three frames for your cartoon by inserting a table with one row and three columns.

5. Position the cursor so it is in the first cell and then choose a picture to insert. Click INSERT, then PICTURE, then FROM FILE: this will open a list of your files and you can select the picture you want.

6. Resize or crop the picture by dragging on the corners.

7. Add the other two pictures in the same way.

8. To add speech bubbles or thought bubbles, click AUTO SHAPES. This option is often placed at the bottom of the screen (see Figure 7). You can also access this option from the toolbar by clicking INSERT and selecting AUTO SHAPES.

Figure 7: Screenshot locating auto shapes in Microsoft Word

9. Choose CALLOUTS (which are basically speech bubbles) from the auto shapes menu; select the shape you want and it will appear on your page. Drag it to the place you want and enter the text in the speech bubble.

10. Print out when finished.

Result

You will have a short cartoon which can be used to help a young person express how they felt at a point in time in their life. Depending on the young person, this can be used to reflect upon after a period of time has passed, in order to discuss how feelings towards an event and person can sometimes alter over time.

Digital life story work element

This is a fun way to express a range of issues, emotions and feelings. Cartoon characters can say things which may be difficult to attribute to a person. The cartoon format can also help to create humorous angles on incidents. Using photos in a cartoon-like fashion means that people in the young person's everyday environment can be used to carry messages which might be difficult to articulate.

Project 8: Three-minute movie
(3–4 HOURS)

This project guides you through making a three-minute movie – although it will take a bit longer than three minutes to make. The idea is to get the young person to pick a topic which interests them to make a short movie about. Because this project requires the use of camcorders and video editing software, it can provide an ideal way to develop the skills need for the potentially more sensitive podwalk project, which features later in this chapter.

What you need

A computer

Video editing software

A digital camcorder, cameraphone or smartphone

Some photos or images

Depending on the level of skill, this may be a technically challenging project to undertake. For those who are unfamiliar with the skills required, skip to Chapters 5 and 6, as these chapters cover the technical aspects in more detail.

There is a variety of video editing software available and many computers come with software preloaded. For computers that do not have preloaded software, you will need to choose this based on what your computer can use. As a rule of thumb, PCs will commonly use a version of Windows Movie Maker, whereas Macs will use a version of iMovie. If this is unfamiliar territory for you, use this to your advantage as a way to engage with the young person you are working with. This can be particularly helpful if you are asking the young person to use their own cameraphone or smartphone to create the movie.

What you do

- **Discuss what the film can be about:** This is your chance to get the young person to give you an insight into an aspect of their life. Initially, this does not need to include anything from their past or any potentially sensitive issues; giving the young person a chance to choose what to show you about their current situation can be just as important as exploring their past.

- **Movie structure and planning:** Discuss with the young person a basic beginning, middle and end structure for the film. Because of the short timescale of the film, it may be helpful to link these sections to portions of time. Young people who are nervous about being filmed may find noting down a few bullet points or writing a script helpful.

- **Give it a try:** Depending on where and what the young person wants to film, you may need to outline some guidelines for filming in public. If this is the case, see Chapters 3 and 5 for more information.

- **Watch it back:** Having created the sections of film, watch these on the camcorder to check if the young person has all they need. If they are happy, import the footage to the computer. For those using camcorders where it is not possible to review film, import the footage onto the computer and re-record content if needed (for more guidance on this, see Chapter 6).

- **Editing:** Use the software programme to edit or trim any content which is not needed and organise the footage in the desired order (additional options can be included when editing depending upon the software being used; for more guidance, see Chapter 6).

- **Save as a movie file:** Regardless of editing software, when the young person has previewed their film in the editing software they will then need to save the file as a MOVIE FILE. This turns the series of clips and effects into a movie file which can then be transferred to and watched on other computers.

- **Burn to DVD:** For those comfortable with this process, transferring movie files onto DVD can add another element to how these short films can be viewed, with aspects of this viewing discussed in more depth in Chapter 7.

Tip

Film clips are normally easier to watch when the amount of zooming in and out is minimal and the camcorder operator has remained fairly still; however, let the young person experiment and be creative. Recording the same thing or person from different angles changes the perspective of the viewer and can add excitement to a film.

Result

The young person will have created a short movie about a topic that interests them. Whilst undertaking this activity, both you and the young person will have begun to develop or hone the skills needed for the more demanding and potentially sensitive podwalk project, described later in this chapter.

Digital life story work element

Recording in the present can encourage young people to reflect on the present, which can be useful before attempting to look at the past and then the future.[2] The three-minute movie, depending on its content, can provide young people with a record of how they looked, sounded and felt at a particular point in time. As adolescents tend to change quickly due to shifting social expectations, peer group relationships and biological changes, so viewing such a clip only a few months later can encourage young people to reflect on how much they have changed.

Project 9: Podwalk
(1 DAY MINIMUM)

The aim of the podwalk project is to engage young people as tour guides, showing the adult facilitating the podwalk around places they have identified as important whilst sharing stories evoked by being in these places.

What you need

A digital video camera or phone camera

A computer

Video editing software

A DVD rewriter

The podwalk project is introduced here in a similar vein to the previous eight projects, but it is important to note that this is the most technologically demanding and potentially emotionally sensitive project to undertake with a young person. For these reasons, more detailed explanations of the individual elements of a podwalk feature heavily in the remainder of the book, with a host of case studies to highlight key themes and issues. Before undertaking this project, you may wish to read through Chapters 5, 6 and 7: Chapter 5 provides a comprehensive overview of how to introduce and plan digital life story work projects whilst negotiating difficulties, with a particular focus on podwalking, and also illustrates how best to guide young people when creating film content

---

2 Joy Rees talks about the idea of starting in the present to look at the past, re-examine the present and look positively towards the future in *Life Storybooks for Adopted Children: A family friendly approach* (2009).

in public and potentially sensitive places. Chapter 6 describes how to import content from camcorders and digital cameras, introducing a host of options to include in the end product. Chapter 7 discusses what to do with this product from a practice perspective and how to encourage young people to reflect upon the experiences their podwalk DVD relates to.

Tip

We would strongly recommend that podwalk projects which have the potential to be particularly sensitive should not be undertaken with young people without Chapters 4–7 being read first. If this is not possible, it is definitely worth restricting podwalking projects to those young people with whom you have already established a strong working relationship. This project can evoke potentially sensitive emotions, and it is vital to complete it, so ensure that you are familiar with the technology and have sufficient time to undertake it fully.

What you do

- **Preplanning:** Think about where the young person might want to go and potential issues in revisiting such places.

- **Pitching:** When introducing the project to the young person, think about how to make this an appealing prospect rather than a daunting one.

- **Planning:** Because this is the most in-depth digital life story work project in this book, with the potential to stretch over a number of days or different sessions, there is a need to plan where and when filming will take place.

- **Creating content:** This involves travelling with the young person to visit places from their life and encouraging them to share their memories of the places and related relationships. Filming trips may take place over a number of hours and therefore it may be useful to undertake several filming sessions, depending on the time available and the young person's wishes.

- **Editing and production:** Once enough content has been created, import the video onto your computer. As described in previous projects, use the computer's video editing software to trim, delete and organise content into the desired order, adding various digital photos, pre-recorded sounds and short music clips if required. Once this is complete, save the film by clicking a command such as SAVE AS MOVIE FILE (this command will vary according to the software). When the file has been saved, burn it to a DVD, adding additional aesthetic elements, such as a DVD title menu, label and cover.

- **Premières and time capsules:** Whilst the focus throughout this project is on listening to young people and engaging them in reflecting about their experiences, the making of the DVD creates valuable opportunities to encourage the young person to reflect on their past experiences in the podwalk location and the people and relationships experienced there in the past, as well as during the podwalk. These conversations can take place at the "première" of the DVD (watching the DVD on a big screen), but also during the making of the DVD and as the young person reacts to you watching the footage. Films can also act as a "time capsule" for the young person in the future, helping them to reflect on changes in their lives.

Result

The young person will have had the opportunity to take part in planning, filming, editing and producing a DVD about an aspect or aspects of their lives. Moreover, they will have had the benefit of being supported through this process by a caring, sensitive and engaged adult who took genuine interest in learning more about their lives and assisted them in reflecting upon the stories they shared. The DVD marks the completion of this process and the feelings of warmth and support fostered by the process of creating it.

Digital life story work elements

- We all have relationships with people and places. On many occasions, the relationships between people in our lives and the places which are important to us are interlinked. For young people who may have experienced multiple moves and different carers, and can often be denied consistently available relationships with important adults, the role of place in helping them piece together important aspects of their life stories is vital. Places can be linked to memories and important points in young people's lives.

- In revisiting places as tour guides, young people can share and reflect upon positive and negative memories from these places. The sharing of the stories, feelings and emotions that they evoke needs to be carefully supported by the adult undertaking the work with them. This is a highly complex role and one discussed at length in Chapter 3.

Extending the project

Because of the different segments which make up the podwalk project, there are countless ways in which it may be extended, limited only by the imagination of the adult facilitating the work and the young person.

Some ways in which young people have chosen to extend podwalk projects have included incorporating photos, images and additional audio material into their project before burning this onto DVD, creating DVD title menus, or using computer software to create labels and covers.

Chapter 3
Working with young people

This chapter discusses ways to guide and support adolescents when undertaking digital life story work. It begins by outlining ways to negotiate expectations and discusses the core responsibilities of the adult(s) facilitating the projects introduced in Chapter 2. It also highlights common risks when undertaking projects with vulnerable young people, suggesting sensible strategies for managing these. To guide discussions, resources and illustrative case studies from the podwalks and other work undertaken in the original research project are included (as mentioned in the introduction to this book).

Negotiating expectations

Before undertaking any form of digital life story work, there is a need to discuss expectations. One of the central ideas behind this work is that young people should take an active role in reflecting upon the stories they share, with the assistance of a supportive relationship with a worker or carer. This active role needs to be negotiated with expectations on both sides made clear from the outset. Expectations guide the roles of both the adolescent and the adult involved; this is not to say that expectations cannot change throughout a project, but that they need to be understood in relation to the project and established from the start.

The word "expectation" is used instead of "rules" to emphasise the responsibilities of both young people and adult facilitators (the latter discussed in more depth later in this chapter), since rules, as the saying goes, are made to be broken. An emphasis on rules can highlight power differences within supportive relationships as opposed to promoting an ethos of empowerment and partnership. Rules can also lead to confrontation and rebellion. Young people are more likely to agree to expectations if they have helped to outline them.

In negotiating expectations, you must discuss what the digital life story work project will involve from the young person, but also explain what the young person can expect from the project and, in turn, from you as a facilitator. The most important part of digital life story work, above any technological knowhow or professional expertise, is the authenticity and predictability of the relationship between the young person and adult involved. Authenticity means that you commit yourself to the relationship, and also that you have a genuine desire to help. For example, when undertaking a project which requires a commitment over a number of weeks, pick a regular time and day each week (where possible and appropriate) with the young person and stick to it. Echoing the comments of Ryan and Walker (2007), if life gets in the way and you cannot meet an appointment, you must provide adolescents with plenty of notice, in person if possible.

By introducing what adolescents can expect to gain from engaging with a project, small tangible rewards may be a useful starting point. Of course, adolescents, like many of us, are motivated by activities which reward them financially. A good idea is to tie this financial reward to an experience, one also shared with the facilitator and that relates back to the adolescent's engagement with the project, the adult and their relationship.

Obviously, there is a need to move beyond monetary rewards and onto the wider array of benefits young people may gain from this relationship. Spending time with young people one-on-one and being generally interested in them and their stories is ultimately beneficial for adolescents. When discussing expectations, it is important that monetary rewards are de-emphasised as you progress with the projects, as such rewards are unsustainable and may detract from therapeutic ends. The relationship with the adult must become more rewarding. A worksheet to help start discussions with the young person regarding expectations can be found in Appendix 5.

For adolescents with learning difficulties, this process could be made more engaging through using a variety of role-playing activities, for example, swapping coats or hats with the young person in order to talk about each other's perspectives. Such activities could be used to support the adolescent at a suitable level, whilst conveying appropriate expectations in an engaging and entertaining way.

Core responsibilities when supporting and guiding reflections

Like life story work undertaken with younger children, the role of the facilitating adult is vital. As the adult facilitating the project, you will face an endless number of potential responsibilities, with each having different implications for how young people can create, develop and experience ownership over the project and the stories they share. Below are outlined some responsibilities common across a range of life story projects, with suggestions for how this relationship can be supportive and guide reflections.

Role model

In being privileged to undertake digital life story work with young people, facilitators also take on the mantle of role models. This is an informal role and one with which those who work regularly with young people will be familiar.

Young people often emulate the phrases, perspectives, mannerisms and actions of the people they admire. As a role model facilitating digital life story work, it is important that you are aware of the impact your relationship with the young person can have on them. This position is one of responsibility and opens up possibilities to engage young people in talking about other issues, including wider uses of digital technologies and media. You may be able to use different projects to demonstrate and discuss responsible uses of digital technologies. In doing so, avoid clichés and scare stories from the media; instead, if possible, use personal experiences and reflective questions to increase young people's ability to discriminate between safe/unsafe and appropriate/inappropriate use of digital technologies and media.

Audience

In engaging young people to share stories, adult facilitators become audience members. This is an important role since different versions of an event can be told for a range of psychological and/or social reasons. For instance, an individual may choose to tell a different version of a night out to those whom he or she considers to be close personal friends, in comparison to what he or she might choose to tell a work colleague. There are truths we tell to those close to us and truths we tell to those to whom we are not so close. This is not always a sign of someone who wishes to deceive or deny elements of the past, but often occurs as a result of the relationship between the parties.

Looked after adolescents might not be able to easily discriminate between what they should disclose to those close to them, and what to disclose to those less well known to them. Digital life story work is about being engaged in communicating with adolescents via these tools. Its wider benefits include being able to create opportunities to talk to adolescents about discriminating between content appropriate for public and private audiences.

As the facilitator, you need to become familiar with the young person's life, care records and reasons for entering care (a point explored in more depth in Chapter 5). This allows potential areas of trauma to be flagged up and handled sensitively. As an audience member with knowledge of the young person's care record, it is easy to assume that when stories differ from those recorded, the young person must be attempting to mislead you. Fahlberg (1994) suggests that children can often reject certain truths in an attempt to construct a more favourable view of events, labelling this tendency "fantasy thinking".[1] Fantasy thinking may occur during digital life story work projects, but it is important to recognise this in context and reflect upon reasons for the sharing of fantasy elements, and the limitations to what care records can tell us about a young person's life and experiences. This is not to place blame at the feet of those producing such records, but rather a recognition of the difficulty of this task.

In recognising differences between stories told by the adolescent and those told by care records, the audience must balance how, when and if to challenge

---

1 For example, in *Tracy Beaker's Movie of Me*, released in 2004, the central character, Tracy (a looked-after young person), describes her mother as a famous Hollywood actress, later discovering that she is actually a stunt double rather than an actress.

the accounts told. Some fantasy elements may be very noticeable, others noticeable by their absences. Such absences may indicate potentially very sensitive experiences in need of careful exploration. In this case, it may be worth asking questions which nudge the young person into reflecting upon absences in produced stories. Such enquiries need to be considered in the context of the relationship experienced with the young person and the occasion in which this occurs. If this is a relatively new relationship, it may be more appropriate to refrain from pushing the young person towards a potentially sensitive aspect until your relationship with them has developed further. Some projects which encourage young people to reflect upon the telling of stories also embed opportunities for questions to arise spontaneously. It is imperative to assume that absences and discrepancies are potentially sensitive and to proceed carefully. The following case study illustrates how fantasy elements can result from a desire to present the self favourably and from a breakdown of audience/narrator roles.

Case study

Ian (16) lived in a long-term residential home and enjoyed using technology. His involvement with the digital life story research project was tentatively suggested by staff, who cited his volatile behaviour as a reason for caution. Despite this, Ian regularly engaged with Simon (lead author and researcher who acted as facilitator) and took part in a range of projects, including a podwalk.

While creating content for his podwalk project, Ian chose to return to his cousin Stevie's garage, a place he stated he used to visit as a boy with his father. Though the garage was locked, there were motorbikes under covers in front of it. In looking under the covers, Ian identified a motorbike by colour. In this exchange, Simon failed to act as Ian's passive audience by interrupting him and stating the type of motorbike Ian was pointing to. In response to this, Ian claimed that he used to own the motorbike, something immediately questioned by Simon. In response to this continued questioning, Ian claimed that he used to race the bike. Simon continued to question this account, resulting in Ian repeating his racing career claim, linking this to a time before he was admitted into care and then spitting in the direction of Simon's feet.

Why did this escalate? In stating the type of motorbike Ian was describing, Simon failed in his role as passive audience. As the audience, Simon was meant to know less than the narrator. Simon began to disrupt Ian's story, his connection to the place he visited with his father, items he was describing, and the relationships experienced in this place. As a result, Ian began to overcompensate and engaged in what could be described as "fantasy thinking", before marking his territory verbally and physically.

Could this have been avoided? As an audience member, it is important to remember that the narrator (young person) is the expert. Here, what could be labelled as "fantasy thinking" resulted from an unwelcomed interruption from an audience member. If interrupting the young person's account, ask questions which encourage the young person to reflect, as opposed to confirm knowledge you think you may have.

Co-constructor

In undertaking projects with adolescents, the presence of the adult facilitator may need to move beyond the role of audience and instead provide assistance in the construction or making of the story. As mentioned, stories are best understood when they are coherent. When sharing stories about their pasts, birth families and care experiences, stories shared by adolescents may be incoherent, fragmented and missing important details. In viewing young people's entire life as a book, if the chapter contents and the chapters themselves are mixed up, the overall gist of the story will be lost. Having knowledge of a young person's care records can enable the facilitator to provide information which may help the adolescent reflect upon such gaps. This reflection can help them begin to make sense of the parts of their stories, bring together the pieces of these stories into chapters, and sort these chapters into a meaningful order in their overall biographical story.

In this process, the role of co-constructor can assist and gently guide the young person to reorder/fill in gaps in stories by jogging their memory with reflective questions. This re-ordering can be further aided by the facilitator being familiar with a young person's care history. If an adolescent cannot remember the age at which they moved placements or schools, for example, by being familiar with the young person's care history, the adult can help the young person work out the age at which they attended the school. Several helpful strategies are noted below involving time and relationships.

- Time is an important structuring element for any story told and one that care populations can often struggle with. Try to encourage adolescents to structure stories using available temporal landmarks such as birthdays or points in time familiar to them or already present in their stories:

  Was this before or after X?
  How old were you then?

  This may be harder for some; facilitators familiar with care records can help with this aspect by using available information to calculate approximate age. Gaps which remain unanswered provide directions for future information searches. Never leave a gap: once a question is asked, help the young person to find an acceptable answer. If a gap is unavoidable, explain what you have done to try and find an answer.

- Relationships and associations are helpful in creating more detailed narratives. Where gaps emerge, ask adolescents to reflect upon who else was there. Relationships with friends, carers and geographical regions can help jog memories and also be used by facilitators to suggest resolutions.

  Who did you used to hang out with here?
  How did you meet them, were they friends with...?
  Where were they from/where did they live?
  So you came here in 2010 with X?
  *Sorry, I have forgotten – how old were you?**

*When suggesting resolutions to narratives using relationships and/or time, it is also helpful to mix up some details or leave a gap to see if the adolescent corrects the mistake. This approach should be used sparingly and carefully as repeated use may be spotted or interpreted by the young person as you not listening to them; this may disengage the adolescent from the project and possibly damage your relationship with them. This approach is not intended to trick the adolescent, but to check they are still engaged and feel ownership over their stories.

Compassionate listener

As the facilitator, you will need to assist the adolescent in re-interpreting events, relationships and coming to terms with or at least managing a range of complex emotions. Attempts to manage and resolve emotions may mainly take place within the reflective conversations between you and the young person, as opposed to having a conversation which is recorded on digital technology during the project work itself. However, this is driven by individual preferences. Some young people may feel more comfortable expressing painful emotions indirectly to technology and playing the recording to you, or giving this to you to watch; others may approach this differently.

Again, it is worth emphasising that digital technologies are a vehicle for accessing these dialogues – it is the relationship betwen you and the young person that supports reflections and the re-interpretation of painful memories and traumas.

Digital boundaries

The risks of using digital technologies to engage vulnerable adolescents in reflections upon traumatic experiences are important. There remains an understandable degree of nervousness around the promotion and usage of digital technologies in practice. Yet by accepting and promoting the use of digital technologies, new opportunities to engage with a technologically proficient generation of young people can be created. As a residential home manager from the original research project commented:

> We've got to get used to this sort of technology; it isn't going away. It's about people not being so nervous.
> (Holly, residential home manager)

This realisation does not detract from the common risks associated with using digital technologies, or from the need to establish sensible risk management practices.

In the real world, vulnerable adolescents can often struggle to maintain and discriminate between appropriate and inappropriate personal boundaries. On some occasions this may result in their sharing too much with those who may do them harm, and often too little with those trying to help. With this in mind, the following common risks and sensible procedures provide an insight into ways in which you can help young people negotiate digital boundaries. The list is not exhaustive and the relationship is the ultimate protective factor.

Common risk:

- Content created for/by digital life story work project(s) being shared on publicly available websites such as Facebook, Twitter or YouTube.

Sensible procedures:

- Conversations with young people about the possible implications of posting content need to focus on the importance of privacy settings,[2] potential audiences and the sensitivity of the content uploaded. The following case study illustrates one such occurrence.

Case study

As part of a digital life story work project, Kai (15) had scanned in an old photo of herself and a birth family member. Despite discussions advising her to the contrary, Kai chose to upload this photo onto her Facebook profile.

When her request to "tag" the birth family member in the photo was ignored and the photo had attracted several unwanted comments, she removed it.

In working with Kai and discussing her feelings about what had happened and the comments that the photo had attracted, it was decided that it would be best to upload personal photos like these to a digital photo frame and for this to be kept in her room. After she had had time to reflect on her actions, Kai commented that 'the old pictures, I'd like put on here (the digital photo frame) 'cos they're a bit too personal for Facebook.'

Could this have been avoided? In this example, Kai owned the original photo and had a copy of its reproduction. It was clear from conversations with Kai that if she was prevented from uploading the photo in-house, she would do this regardless and that attempts to prevent her from doing so would lead to her relationship with staff becoming distant. It was decided that this should be avoided if possible, as the positive relationship would be needed if and when negative/unwanted comments were received.

Learning points: Adolescents take risks and need to learn from their mistakes. It is important when mistakes are made that supportive relationships are available to comfort, support and guide future actions. Though what happened in this case was a risk, the risk of Kai dealing with these emotions without the support of her relationship with staff members was much more serious.

2 *Social Networking and Contact* (Fursland, 2010) discusses such issues in relation to looked after populations and provides practical information in an accessible and relevant manner.

Common risk:

- Losing created content: the computer breaks/the young person deletes all their projects.

Sensible procedures:

- Before undertaking any digital life story work project, it is important to discuss the need to back-up content created with the young person and that, as the facilitator, you implement strategies to do this regularly.

- Backing up content can be introduced in the guise of needing to protect young people's content from accidental loss due to computer problems/virus or accidental damage. In the original research project, adolescents were informed that it would be very useful if they gave their permission for copies of content to be burnt onto DVDs and stored with their care records. This concept was introduced in the form of a time capsule which they could revisit years later and in case they lost their copies.

- At no point during the original research did any adolescent involved seek to deliberately delete created content. However, this is not to say that it could not happen. Perhaps, in agreeing expectations before undertaking each project, the young person could agree to a week-long "cooling-off period" after which they can discuss deleting content with the facilitating adult.

  Such conversations can also be used to introduce the notion that once something is posted on the internet, it cannot be completely deleted. Clearly, case-by-case complexities persist and resolutions need to be sought in collaboration with the young person, care environment and relationship created.

Common risk:

- People other than the facilitator and young person accessing files created during a digital life story work project.

Sensible procedures:

- Other people accessing files created for digital life story work projects, regardless of intent, is both undesirable and avoidable. As with the storage of sensitive non-digital material, there are certain procedures and privacy mechanisms that can be put in place.[3] These include inbuilt protection capabilities such as creating passwords for computer profiles and removable storage devices,[4] but also removing content from recording devices once it has been copied and backed up appropriately.

---

3 Such mechanisms may already exist for digital content within your organisation and need to be checked before undertaking digital life story work.
4 There are a range of websites which can advise you on the best way to password protect computers and storage devices according to the make, model and software. The website www.ehow.com is a good place to start. Alternatively, there are a range of video tutorials for different devices on YouTube.

Summary

This chapter outlines ways to engage young people and negotiate the safe use of digital technologies with them when undertaking digital life story work. By discussing the expectations made upon both the young people and the facilitating adult, the idea of the relationship being a partnership is introduced. The core responsibilities of the adult facilitator, which include being a role model, audience, co-constructor and compassionate listener, are discussed in some detail. Finally, common risks associated with creating content for digital life story work projects are outlined, with suggestions for sensible procedures to reduce these risks.

Chapter 4

Preplanning, pitching and planning

This chapter introduces and illustrates the need to undertake various aspects of preplanning, pitching and planning. It highlights technological and practice practicalities when undertaking projects, before suggesting ways in which the project can be introduced and effectively pitched to the young person. Finally, important aspects and engagement opportunities when planning projects with young people are explored.

To provide detailed guidance on every possible digital life story work project is unrealistic. Therefore, this and the following three chapters introduce the various phases involved in the actual undertaking of digital life story work applicable to the majority of projects introduced in Chapter 2. In the main, these chapters will draw on examples from the original research study which involved podwalks.

Preplanning: people, places and possible stories

Irrespective of whether you have selected one of the projects outlined in Chapter 2 or created your own, the preplanning, pitching and planning phase forms a vital starting position. The preplanning element begins with the facilitator reflecting upon the people, places and possible stories the young person may come to share during a project, with such reflections informed by their familiarity with the young person and his or her story. The point at which you begin to familiarise or re-acquaint yourself with this story will be dependent on the young person, their situation and any existing relationship you may have with them.

This can begin with reading, revisiting and, where appropriate, updating care records, but it does not end here. You should also aim to talk to relevant social workers, residential workers and foster carers, as necessary. If all you know about the young person is what you have read about them, then beginning to talk to them about life stories is also imperative. In undertaking this reading and (where appropriate) file searches, you need to keep in mind who, where and what the young people may talk about during the project you wish to carry out (this is probably most applicable to the podwalk project). By pre-empting potential characters and stories, you will be better prepared to sensitively support and guide the young person and help reconstruct stories and emotions shared.

Tip

It may be helpful to introduce the idea of talking about oneself in relation to the growth in popularity of celebrity biographies and life story interviews, programmes or publications. It may be worth a trip to the library to borrow the young person's favourite sportsperson's/musician's/artist's autobiography or biography, with those published by former care leavers, perhaps including Fatima Whitbread, Paolo Hewitt, Neil Morrissey or Damian Hirst, potentially particularly relevant. Alternatively, a quick search online should reveal a biography section on the young person's favourite sportsperson's/musician's/artist's official website.

People

Whether or not the young person is known to you, you should familiarise yourself with their care files and records. Such background reading will often quickly highlight the reason(s) the young person first entered care, their age at first entry and those who were deemed responsible. This research is good practice regardless of whether you have known the young person for days, weeks, months or years. Young people often have complex backgrounds and scattered experiences, so it is vital that, when supporting their reflections during digital life story work, you are aware of and familiar with these experiences. You need to understand the nature of any contact the young person has had, or is having, with birth family members/former carers, as well as the importance of this contact to the young person. You also need to appreciate how this relationship may have changed, and may continue to change over time.[1]

Positively, this phase may also enable you to suggest individuals that the young person may be able to visit at a later stage in the project. Again, such suggestions require considered thought and consultation with the young person and the individual in question before contact is made. By talking to potential collaborators, you will be better prepared for managing conversations with adolescents who may insist on visiting people who have been deemed unsuitable. This will also help you to suggest alternative ways of creating content if such difficulties occur.

---

1 Beth Neil has written extensively on the area of contact after adoption. For those wanting to learn more, see Neil *et al*, 2010.

Places

The importance of place may be more relevant to some projects than others; nevertheless, people, relationships and places are connected. Photos of people, for example, can represent relationships, but also the places in which these relationships were experienced. Looked after young people, particularly adolescents who have lived in care for a number of years, will probably have experienced a range of placement moves. Accordingly, previous neighbourhoods and local landmarks may represent a point from which reflections can begin.

When working through files and collaborating with appropriate others, keep in mind the safety of the adolescent. Places need to be viewed in relation to young people's experiences in such places, your relationship with the young person and ability to support them and their stories. For those places deemed too sensitive to visit in person or too far away, free software that provides detailed bird's-eye and street-level views is available, the most popular being Google Earth. This programme provides satellite images and allows users to search any location, zooming in and out as desired.[2] Such software can be used to trigger conversations in a manageable way (a point further explored in Chapter 8).

Possible stories

Alongside people and places which may emerge during the sharing of memories, it is also important to pre-empt how young people will position certain individuals as characters in their stories. Stories are not told devoid of emotion – they may be used to position individuals in the young person's life in a variety of ways. The ability to retell and reconstruct one's story gives the narrator, in this case the young person, the power to place those deemed to be responsible in a psychological position within the story acceptable to them at a point in time.

In considering how young people may recall, share and reflect on accounts, you should try to anticipate how certain truths are told and what these truths allow the young person to accomplish. The capacity and need for you to challenge and/or help edit accounts shared by the young person is complex, but is needed in situations when stories told may hamper transitions into adulthood through containing limiting/fantasy elements. This editorial element is additionally complex since, like many of us, adolescents may choose to present the best of themselves and those whom they love when discussing traumatic experiences. You will therefore need to respond sensitively to the situation, the young person and how the story is told.[3]

In considering how possible stories may be told and the need to assist in the editing of these stories, take guidance from Ryan and Walker, who suggest that adults need to 'be honest, but not brutal' (2007, p. 18), sentiments echoed by Baynes: 'A number of children, given descriptions of their birth families so

---

2 This can be downloaded for free at www.google.co.uk/intl/en_uk/earth/index.html. If you do not wish to download this programme, Google Maps (www.maps.google.co.uk) can also provide street views.
3 You may also want to access supervision to reflect upon and develop ways to sensitively support young people whilst they are telling their stories.

glowing, must wonder why they were removed...such sanitisation is unhelpful for all concerned' (2008, p.43). Remember: it is the young people who have lived the events and have also lived through the difficulties.

By anticipating possible stories, you should pre-empt how the stories and characters within them may be retold. The retelling and sharing of narratives can enable troublesome beliefs about the self, others or a traumatic event to be retold and characters within it repositioned. To achieve what can be a very powerful and therapeutic repositioning of characters, your supportive, sensitive and reflective guidance is essential. Consequently, you must be attuned to areas in which the young person may need help to guide, edit and potentially reconstruct and re-interpret.

Technological practicalities

The next phase of preplanning involves considering technological and practice practicalities. Though relatively brief, this element is particularly important when undertaking a project for the first time.

Regardless of the project selected and irrespective of your previous technological experience, it is important to experiment with the hardware and software to be used. Though this may seem an obvious point, it is also very important. As discussed earlier in this book, there is a need to avoid mistakes, as these can be costly in terms of time and effort, but can also jeopardise engagement opportunities with young people.

This is not to say that mistakes and difficulties will not occur throughout projects, and these can be used to engage and empower young people, since on many occasions they may have the solutions. The point to be made is that serious mistakes can halt young people's engagement with the project. Some obvious mistakes can be avoided through learning by doing. Spending an hour or so undertaking a project yourself from start to finish is priceless experience (and can be fun). This will give you an insight into the experiences of the young person during the project, highlighting potential dilemmas, with the young person and their care history in mind. It also provides you with an array of knowledge to predict and resolve some obvious and yet potentially serious technological difficulties. Though this process may not give you all the answers, such difficulties can provide a starting point to introduce the idea of using digital technologies to the adolescents, as demonstrated in the following case study, which details Simon's (the lead author's) first podwalk.

Case study

When refining the podwalking project and the role of adult facilitator, I decided it would be useful to try it myself with a podwalk around my former local neighbourhood, including my old schools and places I used to visit when I was younger. I contacted my old primary school and gained permission to film around the school during the holidays.

During my podwalk I was able to reflect upon memories, events and relationships I experienced in the school, such as where I used to keep my school bag and the bench my father used to sit on with other parents while waiting to collect me. Many of these memories seemed to emerge from seeing particular aspects of the school and occurred spontaneously, and were recorded for relative posterity by the camcorder. Unfortunately, the 45 minutes of filming I undertook around the school and local area was recorded in high-definition (HD), meaning that the video file was very large. This also meant that the camcorder battery (around 75 per cent full when I started) was flat before I finished. The large file would not fit onto a single DVD, meaning that I had to heavily edit it in a time-consuming process.

Could this have been avoided? Like many users of digital technology, I was keen to run before I could walk. I did not fully understand the storage implications of recording in HD and had not read the instruction manual or explored different recording settings. Whilst the flat battery was not a problem on this occasion as I was filming close to home, this could have impacted upon a podwalk with a young person who had travelled a long way to do filming. I decided to buy another battery and find out how to change the camcorder recording from HD.

Learning points: As this case study illustrates, it is imperative to experiment with unfamiliar equipment before engaging with young people. For those with less confidence, get the young people to experiment with the equipment with you. However, spontaneity only occurs once, and the ability to record, edit and reflect upon spontaneity in meaningful places is vital. If engaging young people to assist you in learning how to use technology, encourage them to film objects which are mundane as opposed to meaningful, so that important stories and reflections will not be lost due to unforeseen technological difficulties. Finally, despite reminding young people to switch off the camcorder when not recording, flat batteries will probably occur, so a fully charged spare battery can be very useful.

Practice practicalities

Demands made upon facilitating adults will depend on the context in which they come into contact with the young person. Those working in residential homes, for example, may find it difficult to undertake certain projects due to institutional restraints including shift patterns, rotas and difficulties in organising transport. Nevertheless, such workers may be advantaged by having access to a large array of support and find it easier to create designated timeslots to undertake projects on a regular basis. It is important to highlight that professional constraints can impact upon projects and these should be thought through before a project to avoid creating conflicts and disappointing young people. This does not mean that workers in certain settings will not be able to undertake certain projects; rather that, before approaching a young person, you need to think through professional constraints and create ways to reduce their impact.

Pitching and planning

Once you have decided on a project, been introduced to or refreshed with the young person's background, stories, relevant previous carers and the young person themselves, and looked over the technology and processes required, you can now pitch the project to the young person and engage them in planning it, both of which are critical for success. The following sections introduce practical ways in which both can be achieved whilst empowering young people to take ownership of the overall project, yet still providing opportunities for you to steer the project's development as appropriate.

Pitching

Vulnerable adolescents (like many young people) can sometimes have developed an inbuilt 'I don't know' or 'I can't be bothered' reflex which needs to be bypassed. This is where pitching a project is indispensable. As mentioned in Chapter 3, when introducing a project to a young person, it is important to negotiate expectations, introducing what the project will require from young people, but also pitching what they can expect to gain from taking part in it. Pitching a project can highlight elements that adolescents will find particularly engaging, which can include using digital technologies in stimulating and creative ways, designated one-on-one time with a facilitator interested in their lives, and the ability to edit, produce and keep the project's various products and other tangible incentives offered. This also provides opportunities for expectations to be introduced, refined and negotiated.

Central to the idea of pitching is your enthusiasm. This is not to say that the thought of engaging young people in discussing potentially traumatic memories should be relished or trivialised in any way, but relates to your enthusiasm about empowering and working with young people, valuing the relationship that such projects should foster. If you cannot be bothered to be enthusiastic about the project, why should the young person?

Planning

Having successfully pitched the idea of a project to the young person, the planning will more often than not begin to occur instantly. The level of planning required will be dictated by the project. Relatively simple projects, such as remaking memories, will require significantly less planning than undertaking a podwalk, for example. However, even in simpler projects there is still an abundance of empowerment opportunities, particularly for those young people familiar with such technology. Additionally, for facilitators who do not own or have access to a scanner, for instance, young people can be engaged to help find free access to such equipment, commonly found at local libraries.

Tip

Organising more complex projects can also be used (if appropriate) to scaffold and support wider learning, whether this is independence agendas or key skills such as project management. Such tasks can be particularly useful for engaging adolescents with learning difficulties, since their engagement in the planning process can be supported to an appropriate level. For instance, whilst planning filming trips for his podwalk, Phil (15), used the internet to research train timetables and ticket prices for an adult and student day-pass. By spotting that it was cheaper to travel at a slightly later time and buy off-peak day returns, Phil was also able to budget for lunch.

Independent of the level of planning, it is important that young people feel involved and their opinions valued during this planning phase. In some cases this may be the first involvement young people may have with working with adults using digital technologies in this way, therefore it is important that they feel empowered and have their opinions valued from the start. Being involved in organising and consulting on arranging travel and other practical requirements also encourages partnership working between the facilitator and the young person.

Summary

By introducing the need to preplan aspects of projects, this chapter outlined how the facilitator should pre-empt the people, places and potential stories that may emerge during young people's engagement with various projects. The chapter discussed how, by being familiar with the young person, their care background, appropriate former/current carers and birth family members, the adult facilitator can listen and where necessary help reconstruct potentially limiting and damaging stories. The complexity and dilemmas of such editing were also highlighted. Pragmatic considerations to reduce technological and practice limitations were explored, before ways to pitch projects and engage young people in the planning of projects were suggested.

Chapter 5
Creating content

This chapter focuses on filming and recording as the main techniques through which digital life story work content is generated, and explores a podwalk project. The chapter illustrates how podwalks tend to develop by providing a practice-orientated commentary, interspersed with practical tips that can feed into good practice. In real time the amount of time spent on each element covered in the chapter may be negligible, yet each is integral to all the projects suggested in this guide, as they promote opportunities for young people's confidence and ownership of the material to develop.

The chapter is structured according to how content creation – in this case, filming a podwalk – often progresses. However, this guidance is not exclusive to filming and has applications to a range of digital technologies and projects. The chapter provides general guidance rather than a rigid structure for how this process should progress, since creating content should be driven by the young person.

Points to consider when creating content

Give equipment to adolescents in safe spaces

When introducing the idea of creating content via digital technologies, it is a good idea to give the young person the equipment to play with in a safe space, i.e. a home environment or a place away from members of the public. Enabling young people to play with the recording equipment helps to increase familiarity (in some cases), confidence and a sense of ownership before creating content for real. This is important because it allows adolescents to develop a sense of responsibility for the equipment, and gives them a chance to practise filming if they choose to.

Tip

Many digital technologies such as digital cameras and camcorders now feature LCD screens which enable filmed content to be instantaneously viewed, so users can check its quality.

Reinforce expectations and responsibilities

Whilst creating content in safe spaces may be less sensitive than filming in public, this activity does provide an opportunity for you, as the facilitator, to reinforce the young person's expectations and responsibilities when using digital technologies. In the original research project, adolescents were reminded that their peers and staff members may not wish to be recorded, or have their pictures taken, and they were asked to reflect on how they would feel if another young person or staff member started to record them or take their picture without their permission. This is also a crucial issue to consider if you will be filming in public spaces.

Coach the young person

Spending some time experimenting with creating content in safe spaces also allows you to coach the young person in using the equipment in a manner which gives them the best chance of creating a pleasing finished product.[1] Whilst the product created is a secondary consideration to the building up of a supportive relationship during a project, adolescents will probably want to create a product which they like and are happy to show to appropriate others. Coaching also allows you to reinforce responsible usage and the rights of others not to be recorded. Because of the risks and potential complexities of creating content in public, this is considered in more depth later in this chapter.

Tip

Once a young person is familiar with the basic ways to operate the equipment, it is important to reinforce how to turn it off and safely store it. This puts the young person in charge of the equipment and gives them responsibility for it.

Consider possible roles when creating content

When considering how digital technologies are used across a variety of projects, a number of possible roles for the young person can emerge, with each role potentially impacting upon how he or she will share stories. For a project which may make use of more static recording equipment such as webcams, the impact of these differing roles is fairly minor, as the young person will often act as the on-screen narrator as well as the director, choosing what and how to tell. In this scenario, you may act, for example, as an invited on-screen guest playing the role of interviewer. However, in projects such as podwalking, which uses more mobile devices, the differing roles that you may be called upon to play can be

---

1 Appendix 4 provides practical guidance for how to correctly use filming equipment.

instrumental in how stories are created, shared and reflected upon (as case studies later in this chapter demonstrate).

From a practical standpoint, when using camcorders in projects, it is important to keep in mind that the majority of these devices have built-in microphones that vary in quality and which are not always able to pick up dialogue from speakers who are far away from the camera. This means that it may be better for the young person to remain in the role of director and control the equipment from behind the lens, rather than appear in footage themselves, which risks their voice not being recorded well.

Tip

For young people who want to be on camera in projects that take place outside, there may be a difficulty in picking up dialogue clearly due to distance or background noise. This can be dealt with by the young person recording a retrospective audio accompaniment for these sections to replace any disrupted audio (explained in more detail in Chapter 6). This means that the young person can use their voice to create accounts for the visual elements of the environment they filmed.

From a practice perspective, this decision needs to be driven by the young person, since if they want to be physically present in front of the camera, then this is their choice. Obviously, there is a need to balance the practical elements of creating content alongside the empowering ethos of digital life story work projects, yet highlighting this does not make the balancing of these elements any easier. The following case study highlights how difficult it can be to balance empowering young people and at the same time remaining sensitive to their needs and requests.

Case study

In undertaking a podwalk around his local neighbourhood, Billie (15) was reluctant to play the role of camera operator. Instead, he preferred to stand off camera, narrating and directing Simon (the facilitator) to film his story.

Realising that he was unable to move the camcorder quickly enough to correspond to parts of Billie's story and aware of Billie's dialogue becoming lost, Simon tried to persuade Billie to hold the camcorder whilst sharing stories. Initially Billie refused, instead providing more directions. Ironically, this disrupted Billie's story even more and he became increasingly frustrated, before agreeing to take control of the camera. Almost instantaneously, his dialogue became more confident, descriptive and enthusiastic, and his story more coherent, since he no longer had to provide directions about camera-work. Billie was able to reminisce and share stories about the places visited, while Simon could now concentrate on assisting him and supporting his reflections.

Learning points: On this occasion, by admitting that he was a "useless" cameraman, Simon was able to persuade Billie that he was unable to keep up with his story. This benefited the story and product as now pictures corresponded to words, and allowed Simon to concentrate on supporting Billie and his reflections. Nudging and negotiating with young people so that they take control of digital technology needs to be handled sensitively and informed by the young person's level of need. Facilitators must judge when to nudge and when not to.

Nurture creativity

The potential roles of narrator, director and camera operator can be very fluid, but once empowered to take the lead, young people's creativity should be nurtured and encouraged. Facilitators need to be able to "go with the flow". There are numerous benefits available when young people become empowered to take the lead, as the example taken from Billie's podwalk illustrates, but attempting to persuade reluctant young people needs to be pursued carefully.

Using Billie's case study as an example, he did not agree to become the camera operator until around halfway through filming, nor was he interested in taking responsibility for the camcorder; rather, his engagement was to be on his terms. By going with the flow and being sensitive to how Billie wished to engage, the relationship moved beyond confrontations and the facilitator was able to cajole him into playing a more active role. This led Billie to show more glimpses of himself, with such instances used later to encourage self-reflection.

There is a lot to be gained from young people taking charge during filming. This may not always see them directly controlling the digital equipment, but rather controlling their use of it for creative purposes. It is important to remember that each project presents a range of opportunities for a young person to play a variety of roles in front of and/or behind the lens. The following case study shows how, on her podwalk, Abby was able to creatively switch between directly and indirectly controlling the camcorder and being behind the lens and in front of it.

 ## Case study

Abby (16) undertook two filming sessions for a podwalk, the first at her residential home, and the second at her school and best friend's house, around 40 miles away.

During the second of these sessions, Abby's key worker had arranged permission for her to film around her school. This was particularly poignant for Abby since she had been at the school for three years and was about to leave it to start college. She controlled the camcorder and gave a guided tour around the school, sharing memories and anecdotes. Before leaving, Abby chose to appear on the film next to the school gates, which featured the school's name and logo. Instructing her key worker to hold the camera, Abby stood next to the gates and, in a similar style to that of a news reporter, delivered a short piece to camera, reflecting on her time at the school, the friends and teachers she had met as well as setbacks and progress she had made whilst there. She finished this section by saying it was now time to leave, sharing her anxieties and excitement about starting her college course.

Learning points: At no other point did Abby appear in front of the camera's lens; she appeared to be much more comfortable behind it. During editing and producing her podwalk DVD, the facilitator asked her why she had recorded this section in this manner, to which she replied, 'It just felt right, like it was time to leave so this was me leaving.'

Managing risks when creating content in public

The unprecedented flexibility of digital technologies and the ability to edit the material in a range of programmes only adds to the vast range of creative possibilities that such technologies present. One potential aspect which can blunt creativity is a lack of self-confidence. Perhaps not surprisingly, creating content in public may inhibit the willingness of adolescents to play an active role. Because of the various risks and responsibilities of using digital technologies with vulnerable adolescents in public, below are outlined some good practice points for managing risk to all parties and allowing youg people to create content in public.

Risk: Self-conscious adolescents

When planning projects, it is worth keeping in mind the days and times of visits undertaken to various places. In places where the filming is less sensitive, it may be useful for the facilitating adult to hold the recording device close to the young person, whilst the young person narrates and directs. It may be practical to return to the area at a later stage for more filming, or the facilitator could film the area, with the young person dictating the audio accompaniment at a later stage.[2]

Risk: Members of the public present in the filming area

Members of the public may be present in places young people wish to film. It may be useful to ask permission to create content, for instance, if the members of the public will be caught on film. When this is not practical, ensure that the young person is focused on the area rather than on individuals.

Risk: Uncooperative members of the public

As frustrating as it may be if the young person is prevented from filming by members of the public, it is important to remember that you are a role model for the young person. It is important to comply with the wishes of the individuals in question and empathise with their position and right to refuse to be filmed. It may be worth explaining that the project is for a young person who moves around frequently, that the filming will be brief, and that the content is not for public consumption.

2 For more guidance, see Chapter 2 and the skills listed in the soundscape project, or Chapter 6, which explores times when adding separate audio material.

Tip

The following questions may be useful when discussing with adolescents about filming in public and how to approach potentially unhelpful members of the public.

- How do you think people will feel if they see you filming them?

- If you/your little brother or sister were in the park/street/road and somebody was filming you without asking your permission, how would you feel? And what would you say?

- What do you think we should do if people are in the places we want to visit/film today and why?

Risk: The young person wishes to visit a place which it has been decided is unsuitable

This is particularly difficult and having a detailed knowledge of the young person's care history, knowing them well and having built up a trusting relationship with them is vital. It is worth keeping in mind that if a young person intends to visit a place, more often than not they will find a way to get there, regardless of whether they are "allowed" or not. Such unsupervised visits will inevitably be much more risky than a supervised one.

Bearing in mind that young people may have been denied visits to places from their recent or distant past, extra effort should be made to facilitate visits to places they are able to visit. You may wish to adopt a more ad-hoc approach to gaining permission to film in certain places, with locations that may be prohibited being checked out in advance and arrangements made accordingly, to avoid disappointment for the young person.

Software such as Google Earth could be used to virtually visit places in which filming/trips are not practical or have been deemed inappropriate.[3]

Case study

Lizz (15) lived at the Bridge Street residential home. She enjoyed technology, with her skill and interest being frequently noted by members of staff. The day before the first of two planned filming sessions for a podwalk with Simon (facilitator) and Maurice (staff member), Lizz had been informed that she was to be moved to another residential home due to her behaviour. Amongst the places Lizz wished to visit were areas near to where her former foster carers and her mother lived, both of which were deemed off limits by Lizz's social worker.

In visiting areas unfamiliar to Simon and Maurice, Lizz was in charge of providing directions to the driver (Maurice). Having directed the car into a housing estate, Lizz began to share stories. It quickly became clear that Lizz had directed the

---

3 For more information and discussion around the use of such tools, see Chapter 9.

car onto the street where her former foster carers lived, a place she had lived for around a year. Although she asked to get out of the car and go and knock on the door, Lizz remained in the car, sharing stories about her former carers and her time in the area. No filming was undertaken. After five minutes of sharing stories, Lizz directed the car to a different area which was a short walk away, and began to do some filming.

Learning points: By being denied the opportunity to see her former foster carers, for whatever reason, Lizz had been denied an opportunity to create some closure in this relationship. After this filming trip had finished, Simon and Maurice collectively breathed a sigh of relief and yet each reflected that they would probably do it again.

In this case study, had Lizz not visited this area, she could have missed out on a potentially positive experience, coming at a crucial time for her, since she was shortly to move to another residential home, leaving behind friends, staff and fellow residents. If such moves are not marked by some form of ritual, as Ryan and Walker suggest (2007), young people's moves can blur into each other and hamper a sense of identity and coherence. If an individual does not have a chance to close a chapter of their life story, how can they be expected to start a new one?

Risk: Young person becoming distressed

By physically or psychologically visiting places from their past, young people may become distressed. This is not surprising but it is important to remember that the young person chose to revisit the place in which they became distressed. The process is driven by the young person and so is the sharing of stories. When revisiting a place and sharing stories which may cause them to become distressed, young people will probably need a facilitator to help them create closure, and to listen to and comfort them.

No one likes to see a young person in distress, but you are there to comfort them and enable them to feel safe in the location. This may also be the first time anyone has taken the time to listen to the young person's version of events or the first time they have shared them. This reinforces the importance of being familiar with the young person's story and pre-empting the support you may need to provide.

If young people have these unresolved emotions or traumas, it will be more helpful to the young person if they are listened to and helped while in care, rather than simply having their problems "managed" until they leave care.

Case study

Alice (18) was coming to the end of her time in the Gateford Road residential home. She saw the chance to undertake a podwalk as a way for her to say thank you and goodbye to the staff team that had looked after her since she was 15 years old. During filming for her podwalk, Alice, Simon (facilitator) and Carly (staff member) visited many places, including the home of a member of her birth family (Auntie Jean).

During this visit, Auntie Jean told stories and anecdotes from Alice's childhood and recalled how the six-year-old Alice would race to the door every Friday dinner time, when another member of her birth family would bring her a Cornish pasty. She remarked how much Alice looked like this relative when he was 18. Alice became upset, saying how much she missed her relative and how she was angry and hated him, and went on to detail how she had been in the house when she had heard of the relative's death, and how being in the house reminded her of the funeral service.

Learning points: Clearly, for Alice, revisiting Auntie Jean's home and being compared to her deceased relative reawakened grief, anger and sadness. Such emotions are part of mourning the death of a loved one. The podwalk trip provided her with an opportunity to renegotiate the particular traumatic elements of the story within the relationship she shared with Carly (staff member). Despite being familiar with her care records, this unresolved grief took Carly by surprise and prompted her to do some more work with Alice in this area.

When is enough content, enough content?

Though there is no set limit on the volume of content which can be created for each project, you should remain aware of the timescales available, the aim of the project and whether the process is still engaging the young person. Discuss with them when it is time to move from creating content for a project on to editing and production. Due to the flexibility of the technologies used, extra content can be created at a later point if necessary and edited into existing projects. The creating content phase is likely to reach a natural endpoint from which editing and production will flow.

Summary

This chapter has considered creating content and, more specifically, how podwalks tend to progress. The importance of giving equipment to adolescents in safe places, reinforcing expectations and responsibilities and coaching of adolescents are covered, along with the potential roles which may emerge when creating content, as well as ways to nurture young people's creativity and sensible practices for managing common risks.

Chapter 6

Editing and production

Regardless of the project undertaken, working towards an end goal creates many opportunities to engage adolescents in reflecting about the stories they share. These reflections need to be sensitively supported so that the stories can become integrated coherently into the young person's overall life story. In some cases, this may mean that young people need help refining their overall story, possibly highlighting areas of their past in which further projects and/or sensitive support are needed. Importantly, these reflections must eradicate self-blame and encourage young people to look forward positively towards their futures. This phase is about encouraging young people to recognise their own resilience, effectively turning 'if only this hadn't happened' into 'despite all these things that have happened to me'.

This chapter explores editing and production of digital life story work content, and is structured according to the step-by-step technological process needed to create a podwalk DVD. General technological guidance is provided alongside practice tips which aim to help young people reflect and, where appropriate, re-interpret stories in ways which highlight their resilience and self-esteem. Additional technological terms associated with editing and not covered in earlier chapters are explained in Table 4 in Appendix 2.

Preparing a computer for editing content

System requirements

If you are purchasing new equipment or intending to use unfamiliar equipment, it is vital that your computer can run the digital devices and software required. System requirements can be found on the manufacturer's webpage as well as on the packaging. To check if your computer meets the minimum system requirements for your needs, go to the START menu, right click COMPUTER and select PROPERTIES from the pop-up menu. If these commands do not work for the computer you are using, try entering the search term: 'How can I check what my computer's CPU and OS are?' into a search engine such as Google, making the search more specific by entering the make and model of your computer. If in doubt, consult a retailer or independent consumer guide such as *Which?*.[1]

Installing software

This is particularly important when using more complicated equipment such as camcorders as some will require specific programmes to be installed on the computer you are connecting them to. Commonly, digital devices will include this software preloaded on an accompanying CD-ROM. The device's instruction manual will provide step-by-step guidance on how to install this software. Alternatively, some devices will be "plug and play", meaning that once connected to a computer, the device itself will instruct the computer how to proceed. Other devices may require the computer to be connected to the internet so that the most up-to-date version of the software can be downloaded from the manufacturer's website.

It cannot be stressed enough the importance of referring to the device's instruction manual. Some devices will request that they are plugged into your computer before installing software; others will ask you to do the opposite. Helpfully, more and more manufacturers provide a range of useful online materials. You can also search for online tutorials (YouTube has many of these) and could maybe ask the young person to assist you.

Preparing content

Below, we outline a series of practical steps to prepare content for editing, including transferring files from digital technologies onto computers from which editing can begin, and where necessary converting files into those compatible with the computer/editing programme being used. Please note: this is only general guidance, due to the vast array of technologies and programmes readers will have access to.

Transferring digital files

Transferring content such as pictures, audio files or video files will require you to connect the digital device to your computer. If you are unfamiliar with the technology, refer to the instruction manual or YouTube. By searching online for: 'transferring video files from (insert make and/or model of device, e.g. camera or camcorder) to (PC/Mac[2])', you can access numerous helpful YouTube tutorials.

---

1 If you get stuck, visit www.which.co.uk/technology/ which has a number of accessible guides.
2 If you are using a PC, you will probably be importing into Windows and editing in Windows Movie Maker; if you are using a Mac, you will be importing into Mac and editing with iMovie.

Tip

Transferring content from digital devices can be time-consuming and dependent upon a range of factors including size and type of content, as well as the speed of the computer. You may find it helpful to transfer content from the device onto the computer and/or editing programmes before sitting down with the young person to get started, both saving time and ensuring that the young person will be attentive when reviewing and editing content. This can be particularly helpful when time with the young person is limited or for young people with a particularly short attention span.

Where time is less of an issue, it is still important that the young person comes to the editing and production process in the right frame of mind. Starting to transfer data and then leaving the computer to finish the process unsupervised may be helpful, as long as the computer is safe and content remains private.

It is important that all the content is transferred, that it is also left on the digital device, if possible, and that a backup copy is saved on the computer. This ensures that should anything go wrong, the original content is not lost.

Converting files

Digital devices store data in a range of file types, dependent upon the content (e.g. picture, audio or movie) and the manufacturer of the device itself. Converting files involves changing the file type so that it will run in the desired editing packages. This may not always be necessary as newer digital devices and editing programmes tend to produce more compatible file types. But you will not know for sure if your editing software or media player will support the file types your devices create without trying it out first, reinforcing the need to practise this step using "practice" content before working with the young person.

Editing content and stories

Once you have prepared the computer and have transferred content to it, now you need to prepare the young person. Talk to them about this process and how they can stop at any time to have a break if they wish. Empower young people to take the lead and operate the computer where possible – you may need to encourage them to do this. Sometimes this can be difficult, but it will be beneficial for the young person to engage with the task on their terms.

Case study

Trying to motivate and empower Billie (15) during the filming phases of his podwalk (see Chapter 5) was not a simple process. There are many shades of grey between engaged/empowered and unengaged/powerless. When Billie was persuaded to control the camcorder during filming, this was to be on his terms, and this trend continued into the editing phase of his podwalk.

Following Billie's podwalk, the editing process was to begin a week later with Simon (facilitator). Billie was accompanied by Polly (staff member from his residential home). Having already transferred the content Billie took during his podwalk onto his PC into a folder marked BILLIE'S PODWALK, everything was ready to go.

By getting Billie to switch on the PC whilst he talked to Polly about the podwalking, Simon put Billie in prime position to take charge of the PC from the start, a position which Billie was keen to avoid by banging on the computer keys. Improvising, Simon bet Billie 50p that he could not go through the rest of the session gently operating the keyboard and mouse, a bet which Billie accepted and eventually won.

Learning points: Billie was reluctant to take control of the computer so using excessive force on the keyboard became a way to encourage someone else to undertake the editing process. It was important to positively recognise, reinforce and encourage Billie's engagement, which freed Simon to sensitively support Billie on the practical and emotive side of editing content and stories during this phase. In this case, 50p was a small price to pay.

Opening a new project

When opening editing software, the default settings mean that the programme opens up a "new project", a "scrapbook" space where you and the young person can edit and move content around without effectively gluing it in place. This gluing, or rendering, takes place towards the end of the production process.

Open a new project and move content into it – most commonly, by "dragging and dropping" the content imported onto your computer into the editing programme, as shown in Figure 8.

Figure 8: Screenshot illustrating content imported into a project from a folder

Editing sections of content

Having imported content into a project, you can now edit it. This will probably involve viewing a clip in a "timeline" view and "trimming" sections of the clips as desired. The timeline view shows the length of the imported clip and allows you to edit out unwanted sections according to differing time points, as shown in Figure 9. Some software will only allow you to "trim" a clip from its beginning or end; others will allow you to split the clip into different sections, meaning it can be edited multiple times.

Figure 9: Screenshot showing a timeline view of a single clip with editing options

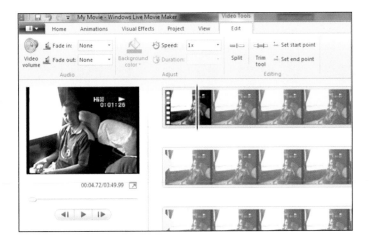

There are a wide variety of editing programmes available, which all operate in slightly different ways. Practise using the software before working with the young person, perhaps seeking additional guidance from the host of online tutorials available on YouTube. The search term: 'How to edit the video in...' and 'video editing tutorial' should locate these.

Pictures can also be included in film clips. The editing of photos will usually take place in a photo editing programme. Many share the similar basic functions, including features such as rotate, red eye removal and cropping, as covered earlier in Chapter 2.

Editing stories

The editing of content has implications for how stories come to be told and re-told. In many ways, this is a dual process: editing content requires you to support the young person's use of editing software, whereas editing stories requires you to sensitively support the young person's reflections and their interpretations of their shared stories.

In comparison to conventional life story work, digital life story work requires a realisation and acceptance that adolescents have a stake in how their stories are told. This is not about creating false truths or endorsing "fantasy thinking"; it is about appreciating that there is more than one way in which a story can be told. It is important to ensure that young people do not rely upon limiting stories and interpretations of life events. You should also encourage young people to recognise their own resilience in the stories they tell, turning 'if only this hadn't happened' into 'despite all these things that have happened to me'. Where relevant, you may also need to emphasise young people's blamelessness for their situation, repositioning characters in stories whilst highlighting young people's ability to influence their own futures. This can be complex, but it is important that we recognise it is not impossible.

On occasions during editing, young people may seek to delete or heavily edit content. This is particularly challenging and yet creates an opportunity for exploring the meaning of the content. Asking the young person why they are editing, trimming or deleting certain sections may seem obvious but it is important to ask rather than assume. Asking a question immediately allows you to follow up and further explore the answer given.

Being able to edit out or delete an individual from content at a point in time may also be cathartic for the young person. This is where the ability to create backup files or retain the content on the digital device for some time is particularly advantageous. As mentioned in Chapter 3, it is vital that the young person is aware of the backup copy and is able to access it following a cooling-off period. Here, you must balance empowering the young person to take the lead in the process against acting in a way which you believe is in the young person's best interests at that point in time.

Ordering sections of content

The ordering of content may have already occurred naturally when importing and editing. However, there are different ways in which content can be ordered. From a technological perspective, sections of content can be reordered by dragging and dropping clips into a different order in the timeline view (shown in Figure 10 below). From a digital life story work perspective, the ordering of content may emphasise the differing aspects and purposes of the project. Using the podwalk as an example, content could be ordered in accordance with the order in which it was created, if the aim of the podwalk was to emphasise the experience of

Figure 10: Screenshot showing re-ordering sections of content by "dragging and dropping" in timeline view

creating content. Alternatively, content could be created in relation to the young person's chronological experiences, with the most distant appearing first and the most recent appearing last. Such ordering and the reasons for it need to be explored with the young person.

Saving the project

It is a good idea to save the project at this stage. Obviously computers can go wrong, and periodically saving work ensures that all the effort the young person has put into the project will not be lost. Additionally, saving a project before the production phase provides a natural opportunity for a break in the process, which is advisable if the editing process has been particularly long. This allows all parties time for reflection before revisiting the saved project afresh and progressing into the production phase.

Production

The advantage of using digital technologies to create digital life story work products is that it is fairly simple to create a crisp product by using a variety of free software. The production phase is very much about allowing the young person's creativity to flow and enabling them to increase the aesthetic appeal of the product if they wish. Here, general guidance is given as to what can be included, covering a host of skills needed in various projects, but focusing on those needed to create a podwalk DVD.

Cinematic appeal

When attempting to add aesthetic appeal to a digital life story work product, it is important that the underlying purpose and process behind the project is not lost. Essentially, this is a very important, sensitive and potentially therapeutic piece of work. As with more traditional life story work, the way the product looks is of secondary importance to the process and relationship with the young person that are created/strengthened by undertaking the work.

- **Title:** Titles tend to be added to the beginning of a movie file but can also be inserted into other places where desired; for example, a young person might want to add a title to introduce a person or scene in their film. In many editing programmes, text is added in a similar way to conventional text-based documents, with users able to alter font size and style as well as background.

- **Captions:** These can be overlaid and displayed in various places on the screen. They can be particularly useful in helping young people associate names, faces and places but can also denote the dates on which the filming or photo was taken. They can be used inventively to support young people with a range of different needs: captions can be used as subtitles to support young people from a range of different cultural backgrounds by displaying spoken words in English or another language; subtitles can be used to assist young people with a range of hearing or speech difficulties; and can also support the engagement and ownership of young people with learning needs.

- **Transitions:** This is the term for graphics that appear between clips or pictures: essentially, they control how a film moves from one video clip or picture to the next – for example, one picture can be faded out, whilst another is faded in. Like all of the options listed here, the user can control how quickly or slowly transitions fade in and out.

- **Effects:** Many software editors allow you to choose from a range of special effects that can be added to the film; for example, for a part of the film which a young person might want to appear more distant in time, certain programmes have a special effect that will make a clip look like an old-time movie.

- **Credits:** In a similar fashion to titles, credits are typically placed at the end of films, often moving slowly from the bottom to the top of the screen and listing those involved in the film's creation. Young people often enjoy adding credits to their film, allowing them to thank the people who agreed to and participated in their filming. This can also add fun to the proceedings by enabling young people to thank those "involved" in lighting, wardrobe, hair and make-up, as well as providing an opportunity for any bloopers or outtakes which they may wish to include on the DVD but were not suitable for inclusion in the main film.

Tip

Adding audio to a film in the form of voices can enable appropriate previous carers, birth family members or teachers to speak about their relationship with the young person and their fondest memories of them. This audio file could accompany photos of the speaker or of them with the young person. This needs to be approached on a case-by-case basis and should focus on the positive aspects of such relationships, as opposed to why these relationships may have broken down.

- **Additional audio:** Adding additional audio to a film can increase the young person's sense of ownership of the project or process, and also influence the "feel" of the finished film.

- **Voice:** If a young person's voice on the film has been lost due to background noise, a retrospective audio accompaniment/audio story can be achieved by the young person watching back their clip and retelling the story whilst being recorded. However, the young person may not remember what they said at the time, and the voices of those also present in the clips will be lost.

- **Music:** Adding music to a young person's podwalk can be very popular with young people, although the volume level may have to be negotiated with the facilitator. Phil and Billie (both 15) insisted on being able to include snippets of music within their podwalk DVD. Phil (15) selected a small extract of a favourite track and edited this so that it faded in slowly at the end of one clip, remained whilst the caption introducing the next clip was shown, and then faded out once this clip started. This can be relatively easy to achieve, and is something that young people will enjoy doing.

Save project as a movie file

Once the young person is happy with the edited project, re-save the file and then preview it in full-screen before saving it as a movie file – this may take anywhere from two or three minutes to up to two or three hours, depending on the complexity of the file and speed of your computer. This provides you with an ideal time to have a break from the process if necessary. You can play the movie file on your computer's media player, and also on different computers if appropriate.

 Tip

To check if your computer has DVD making software, the following commands may be useful:

Open START MENU, *in the* SEARCH PROGRAMMES AND FILES *box and enter the word* DVD. *This will search the computer's files and flag up any programmes or files with DVD in their title.*

 Tip

Transferring a movie file to a DVD is known as "burning" and requires that your computer has some form of DVD making software and a DVD writer. The CD/DVD drawer on the computer will probably have a logo or sticker which reads 'DVD R/RW' or something similar. If you are still unsure whether the computer has DVD making software/a DVD writer, insert a blank DVD, open it in MY COMPUTER and try to copy/paste files into it, clicking WRITE FILES. If the software is not present, you will see an error message.

Creating a DVD

The final element of the production process – burning the saved movie file onto a DVD – may not always be necessary. The difference between burning a file to DVD and simply keeping it as a movie file is that movie files can be more readily edited, deleted and shared. In comparison, once something has been burned to DVD, it remains a stable representation of the process undertaken since it cannot be readily manipulated. Also, with the young person's permission, DVDs can be stored with their existing care files.

There are three different steps to creating a DVD:

1. **Creation of the movie file:** This has already been covered in the previous section.

2. **Rendering:** You will need to open DVD making software. There are a number of free downloads available but it is worth checking if your computer has this software already installed. The rendering process can be understood as the

"gluing" of contents onto the DVD – after this process, the film on the DVD will be permanent and uneditable. When rendering, you create the DVD's title menus, insert chapter points and select music to play during display of the title menu. Although this process may seem a little irrelevant and time-consuming, these extra touches can really make a difference to the finished product, turning any project into one which the young person can be proud of. This process can be accomplished fairly quickly. On a final note, help the young person double-check the text of the title menu and chapter points if necessary.

Figure 11: Screenshot showing an example of a DVD title menu

3. **Burning to DVD:** Once the young person is happy with the DVD menus and has previewed what these will look and sound like, you can burn the finished product to a DVD. Follow the process as guided by the DVD making software you are using.

Extending the project

For those who feel more adventurous and have the available equipment, there are programmes which can create and print DVD and CD labels and the inlays for covers (see Figure 12 overleaf). The images in Figure 12 show some of the possibilities of using the free-to-download trial Disketch DVD/CD label inlay making software. The software downloaded for free to create this label was from www.nchsoftware.com/labeler. Some features of the software are unavailable unless you are willing to purchase the full package. These are very much peripheral final touches but may add to the 'Wow, I did that!' factor.

Finally, this is an ideal opportunity for you, as the facilitator, to ask the young person if they will allow you to create a backup copy of the DVD and put this on their care files to keep it safe.

Figure 12: Screenshot showing the creation of a DVD label using *Disketch* software

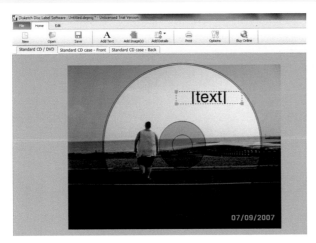

Summary

This chapter has explored the technical and practice features of editing and prod ucing digital life story work products. Case studies highlight important points for consideration around managing the editing process and the possible implications of young people heavily editing content. General advice is also included about burning young people's content to a DVD.

Chapter 7

Completing the project

This chapter explores how completing a project can create an opportunity to bring the process elements of this work, and in some cases the facilitator's relationship with the young person, to a close. The notion of having a première for the film is introduced, to which young people can invite guests to view the product they have created, which in turn gives those present a chance to reinforce and praise the young person's efforts. The chapter highlights the première as a recognisable endpoint for individual projects, but also illustrates how the product can come to act as a digital time capsule, allowing the young person to reminisce about the process and their relationship with the facilitator, which will have been experienced in a richer way than is possible through conventional life story books.

Holding a première

Wow! That looks wicked, I thought it'd look crap but it don't, it really don't.
(Ivy, 14)

When we are proud of something we have done, we often want to show it off to others, and creating digital life story work products such as a photo collage, CD or DVD allows a young person to do this. Importantly, it also gives those around the young person a chance to praise and positively reinforce their efforts, whilst sensitively supporting their reflections and interpretations of the memories and relationships it could represent. Wherever possible, you, as the facilitator, should be present or available immediately after the young person views their product for the first time. If this is not possible, consider rearranging a time to view the product with the young person. Beyond this, you should also contact those who will be present at the first viewing of the film and guide them in how to support the young person through this process. It cannot be overstated how important supporting young people during or after viewing a digital life story work product can be.

Typically, looked after children and young people can struggle to discriminate between when and when not to share sensitive information, and with whom to share it. Some may have such low self-esteem and self-worth that they simply may not care who sees sensitive personal information about them. When a digital life story work product is personally sensitive, those who view it and their reactions can influence how the product comes to be interpreted and re-interpreted by the young person. For many young people, elements of their digital life story work project may be very personal and emotive; therefore who they invite to share it with them should be carefully discussed with them.

A première is the first time in which a film is shown in full; in the case of digital life story work products, these could be invited screenings, private screenings or public screenings. In the original digital life story work project, those young people who opted for private screenings held either "invited" screenings, in which those who the young person selected were allowed to attend, or chose, in the first instance, to view their product in private. Some young people chose to view their DVDs in more public areas, such as the living room of their residential home.

Tip

If the young person wishes to have a première and to invite others to be present, discuss with them the rules of the première, and encourage the others present to think about how they should behave – should they watch quietly, or comment on the product? You could discuss with the young person how they would like their product commented on, or whether they would like to organise a cinema-style "podwalk night" where you could make popcorn together and then watch the DVD.

There are several things to consider when organising a première. An obvious point of caution is the potentially sensitive and personal nature of sharing digital life story work products in a more public way. Though you should respect the wishes of the young person, you must also talk to them about personal boundaries – an issue of particular importance in relation to the possibility of young people uploading products to Facebook, Bebo or YouTube. The case study of Kai (15), who posted an old photo of herself and a birth family member on Facebook, shows that young people do not always listen to those who look out for their best interests. However, they will probably always need sensitive support when things go wrong and assistance in readjusting personal boundaries. The trial and error of personal boundaries in public spaces is not a care-specific phenomenon, but it is typically an area of weakness that looked after young people need help to manage.

Regardless of the type of première, the digital life story work product represents a piece of work which the young person has undertaken and, crucially, completed. This must be recognised by those around the young person, a process which typically begins with listening to young people's initial reactions during and after their premières.

Tip

Double-check that the CD/DVD works in the CD/DVD player you wish to use at the première. Young people can also use a games console connected to the TV to play their projects.

Initial reactions

It is important that those around the young person take the time to listen to what they say during and after they watch their completed product for the first time. For more public screenings, you may also need to manage the reactions and comments of others. However, it is important not to underestimate the warmth and support when products are shared with people the young person feels close to and trusts. Some of those present, including the young person themselves, may need their reactions guided and sensitively explored.

Tip

Beyond any self-deprecating defence mechanism, which you and other audience members may need to help the young person negotiate, première screenings will typically focus more upon the content of the DVD rather than the relationships that the content comes to represent. As the case study with Lizz (15) indicates, more sensitive conversations can take place after screenings. The première is only the start of an ongoing reflective process, a point explored in the time capsule section of this chapter and in Chapter 8.

In the first instance, young people may only highlight aspects of the product that they are unhappy with, for example, a mis-spelt word or the places they were unable to film. This latter aspect needs to be greeted with empathy and the young person helped to talk positively about this experience where possible. During her screening, Lizz (15) commented that she was "not allowed" to visit her former foster carers. This comment was not discussed further during the screening but was discussed afterwards, allowing Lizz to vent her frustrations, talk about what she would have filmed and positively reminisce about her former foster carers. Sharing in the emotive content, both sad and joyful, whilst showing empathy and respect to the young person and their stories is vital.

In screenings where only the facilitator and young person are present, more reflective and supportive conversations may take place. Where possible, it is a good idea to let the young person take the lead, with a facilitator supporting reflections when suitable.

If there is one lesson to take away from holding a première, it is that viewing a film is like dropping a stone into a puddle: it creates ripples, and these will stretch beyond the première. An engaged listener is vital in helping young people to talk about their reflections and integrating these into young people's overarching life stories in a coherent way. This point is particularly important when young people choose to have a private viewing of their DVD for the first time.

Private premières do not allow facilitators the chance to immediately reinforce, positively re-interpret or support young people's reflections. As such, it is crucial that you create opportunities to talk to the young person about what they thought of the project. Asking to view the product with a young person creates such opportunities. This may also allow you to assess whether the young person becomes frustrated and/or angry at what they see, maybe even choosing to destroy the DVD. An advantage of digital life story work is the ability to quickly and cheaply recreate the product, as long as you have a kept backup copy.

Time capsules

I think the best thing about what you've done is, a lot of the things you see especially when kids leave care, you can give them a great big box full of stuff, and that'll just get disbanded. There'll be bits flying all over the place. If it's on a DVD and the fact they can go back, revisit stuff again and keep... It's on one very small thing, and they've got everything on it, do you know what I mean? That for me is one of the key things...
(Jez, residential worker)

The première marks the end of the digital life story work process and can be used to create closure in a variety of ways. It can be used to support young people in transitions between placements in care and potentially when they come to leave care. Although the première provides a recognisable endpoint for the digital life story project, it also marks the beginning of its potential longer-term impact. Each time the product is viewed its meaning can be reworked and re-interpreted. In many ways, the product can begin to act as a digital time capsule.

Much like conventional life story books, products created will be revisited and re-watched by young people. The advantage of using digital technologies is that these can enable the life story work process, and the relationship experienced during making the product, in a richer way than life story work books are commonly able to do. As life story work tools, digital technologies record the voices and appearance of those involved in the young person's life and the project at a point in time. They can represent the warmth experienced in relationships and the idiosyncrasies of this relationship. A photo placed in a life story work book cannot fully represent such aspects, meaning they can be forgotten over time.

Reminiscing about one's past and previous relationships is a normal part of everyday living. For looked after young people who may not always be in contact with people with whom they shared these experiences, reminiscing can be much harder. If we consider humans as storytellers, then people with disrupted and potentially traumatic early life experiences may need help in getting their stories started. Digital life story work offers them a more detailed starting point.

The other thing is because you know all these young people are looked after and they go off and they leave ... this area and they'll leave the staff ... and you know they'll be moving onto a life without having ... you know, taking

us with them. You know, it's really nice that they've got that DVD to look back on because most ... young people when they grow up can go back to the family and look at albums and our kids have got to take everything with them...
(Polly, residential worker)

Summary

In highlighting the première as a recognisable endpoint for digital life story work projects, this chapter highlights how such an event can be created and managed by the facilitator. In doing so, you can introduce the young person to the longer term potential of their DVD as a digital time capsule.

Chapter 8

Towards tomorrow: storying the self

This chapter promotes the idea of digital life story work as an ongoing process rather than a series of isolated activities. In undertaking projects with young people, technical skills are developed and shared, which can provide a greater understanding of how technology can be used to assist with reflection, memories and self-understanding. This know-how enables ongoing work and equips young people with ways of thinking and reflecting which may be utilised throughout their lives. This chapter considers two aspects of continuing digital life story work: firstly, how you can continue to expand digital life story work materials by exploring further resources and using them creatively; and secondly, how digital life story work relates to the everyday digital activities of young people and how the use of material of a personal nature may be stored now and in the not too distant future. The chapter also outlines possible future directions for digital life story work.

Safe use of technology

The relationship between you, as facilitator, and the young person developed through digital life story work aims to provide them with a caring, sensitive and engaged audience, whilst supporting them to operate in safer ways when online. The projects undertaken within this supportive relationship will help young people to reflect on and describe their experiences, and to construct new ways of understanding themselves and their circumstances – including how digital technology has been used and can be used. One of the major "problems" of digital technology is that it is constantly changing, offering new and exciting resources, new ways to share information and communicate. Through digital life story work activities, you will build a relationship in which discussions of digital safety are regularly revisited. This ongoing conversation means that currently available and new resources can be accommodated into the young person's life with greater openness.

Wider conversations about appropriate personal and digital boundaries are rooted in aspects of all the projects introduced in Chapter 2, and highlighted further in Chapter 3. In commenting upon the use of technology in child welfare, Tregeagle and Darcy (2008) recognise that this is a challenging area and that the increasing merging of technologies, such as the way in which internet activities can be performed on mobile phones, potentially increases the risks that young people are exposed to. However, they also recognise that socialising and forming relationships is a central part of teenage life and that most young people are heavy users of technology. Not engaging with young people about this subject is therefore not an option.

> I guess kids in care do sometimes have that tendency to be overly open straight away with things and there's loads of free internet hotspots now... you can go to McDonalds and get on the internet, that's not that far away and libraries have free access too...
> (Mark, residential worker)

The online world carries risks, and many young people with whom you work will be particularly vulnerable. Digital life story work projects will not magically cure this. Risky behaviours online, as with those displayed offline, are common manifestations of emotional problems which young people may suffer from, due to how their physical and psychological wellbeing has been affected by pre-care and, in some cases, care experiences. But digital life story work projects and the relationships developed through these do provide a chance to help young people explore and use technology more responsibly and with greater awareness of risk. If we are to help young people to function safely in this digital world, we have to admit that they will occasionally encounter problems. Expecting them to be proficient, or to become proficient instantaneously without support, coaching and encouragement in an area in which their peers who have not experienced significant disadvantages continue to struggle is an unrealistic and unfair expectation.

> I think that the safeguards are only there once they've done something that makes a violation but perhaps we can assist them in not making a violation in the first place...You know it's like...when your kid's learning to ride a bike: do you not bother with the stabilisers on them and let them fall off? Or do you put the stabilisers on first and take them off as they get better?
> (Peter, senior residential worker)

Widening participation

We have suggested nine digital life story work projects in this book, many of which can also be extended as described. But these projects, like the book itself, are only starting points. As technology changes, what was expensive and difficult to do a few years ago can become cheaper and easier. The first cameraphone was prohibitively expensive, but now the number of cameraphones exceeds the number of purpose-built cameras. In a similar way, the diffusion of smartphone technology and a growing secondhand phone market will help to spread this technology. As digital technologies become more accessible, the possibilities of integrating them into existing and new digital life story work projects will increase. Below, we describe a virtual podwalk project, carried out online by using Google Maps.

Tip

On first viewing Google Maps, it can appear complicated, although there are numerous guides available. It may be useful to first assess if the young person would benefit from creating a virtual podwalk using Google Maps, or whether the static images available on this programme would suffice to spark conversations about places viewed.

Virtual podwalk

In situations where it is difficult or impractical to visit certain locations, young people can be supported to undertake virtual podwalks through the internet, and initially through Google Maps. In discussing the logistics of a trip and where they would be able to visit, young people can find free online map software particularly useful. By clicking in the FLY TO box on the left hand side of the screen and typing in places they may want to visit, young people can view their old neighbourhoods. The software allows users to toggle between birds-eye images, maps and buildings. It is simple to zoom close into the map by rolling the mouse wheel forward, or clicking the + on the right hand side zoom slider.

Another option, in Google Maps and Google Earth, is to use Streetview. This allows users to go to street level and "walk" along streets. To go into Streetview, click the orange "pegman" on the zoom slider and, while holding down the mouse button, move the "pegman" to the location you want to view. You can click and drag the mouse around the screen or use the arrow keys to look around. You can return to the map view by clicking on the x at the top right corner of the screen.

The basic applications of Streetview in both Google Maps and Google Earth allow the young person to virtually navigate around places that are important to them, thereby creating a virtual podwalk. By being able to virtually walk around their old neighbourhoods, young people can begin to tell stories in a similar manner to how they would do in an actual podwalk.

Tip

You can download Google Earth for free! Versions are also available for purchase, which allow advanced features such as high resolution saving and printing of images, but the free version will suit most people's needs. There is accessible guidance online including easy to follow video instructions (www. google.co.uk/intl/en_uk/earth).

The usefulness of this approach will differ depending on the young person's circumstances, relationship with you and level of need. Obviously, there are advantages and disadvantages to the virtual aspects of this approach. The disadvantages include young people being unable to touch, hear and smell the familiarities of the places virtually visited. Such disadvantages may impact more on the suitability of virtual podwalking with adolescents with vision impairments and learning difficulties, where young people may be more reliant on tactile, audio and olfactory senses. Pragmatically, stories shared by young people during virtual podwalks, in what can be instantaneous sharing experiences, may not be as easy to record. Using a camcorder to record a young person undertaking a virtual podwalk, with the lens pointed at the computer screen, may create a film with poor picture quality. This should be set up and practised to hone the quality of the film before the young person undertakes their virtual podwalk.

The advantages of a virtual podwalk include the ability to cover huge geographical distances, particularly useful for adolescents who have experienced a series of out-of-county moves, but also for young asylum-seekers. In some cases, by toggling between birds-eye view and Streetview, young people may be able to highlight discrepancies, allowing conversations on how places can change and which view might represent the young person's memories most closely. Google Earth includes an option to look at aerial images taken at different points in time. Additionally, since Google Earth also displays the dates that the images were taken, young people can be encouraged to reflect upon their relationship to the place via the images, and work out if they were living there when the picture was taken.

There are a few things to consider when using Streetview. As the images are collected by a roving camera, it will pick up people who happen to be on the street and other objects such as cars and caravans. As its name suggests, Streetview takes still images of streets and roads, meaning that smaller details such as the paths which connect housing estates may sometimes only be visible by zooming in on certain images.

Google Earth allows you to "placemark" where young people were born, lived and moved. The number of times a young person has moved or the distance they have travelled can be visually represented and talked about. You can also identify where significant others live or come from. If the computer you are using to facilitate the process is shared, you may wish to create a Google account. If you are going to use some of the more advanced features of Google Earth such as "placemark", others accessing this information on a shared computer should be avoided. However, like the majority of internet-based platforms, Google accounts revolve around sharing information with others in the form of online social networks. Before encouraging young people to create accounts, it is worth exploring privacy and security settings. Like all digital life story work, it is best to have a conversation about expectations and plan a way of using the material.

If you are in any doubt about how to protect information, use the various views available in Google Maps and Google Earth in another programme by taking a screenshot (see the box below for guidance). Once saved as an image, screenshots can be used as appropriate and embedded into any of the digital life story work projects.

Tip

To take a screenshot, get the image you want on screen, and locate the PRINT SCREEN/SYSRQ button on the keyboard. Press this, and a screenshot will be taken. Screenshots can be quickly turned into images by pasting them into software packages including Microsoft Word, Paint and various photo editing software. Instructions for doing this using PowerPoint are below.

1. Take the screenshot by pressing the PRINT SCREEN/SYSRQ button and then open PowerPoint.

2. Press the CTRL key and the V key simultaneously to paste your screenshot onto a blank presentation slide. If you wish to crop the image, right click on the image and edit as required.

3. To turn this into a picture file, select FILE and SAVE AS and in the pop-up box search for the SAVE AS TYPE box. Press the left mouse button to reveal a host of options. From this list you can select your preferred image format; our preference is .jpeg.

4. After choosing this option and selecting where you want to save this image, another dialogue box will appear giving you the options for CURRENT SLIDE ONLY or EVERY SLIDE; select the appropriate option.

Sharing digital life story work

As you work together with the young person using digital technologies, the young person may wish to expand their reflections or share products of digital life story work with others, or integrate it with their existing internet usage. The policy and guidelines of your organisation may lay down constraints about what the young person can and cannot do. But mobile technology is now commonplace, so conversations need to occur about what digital life story work material, if any, could or should be shared with others. As a body of digital life story work is created, the young person may feel that some of this would take on greater significance and meaning if there was a wider audience. For young people in general, but especially for vulnerable looked after young people, their digital identity and status may be highly valued.

Social networking websites and content-sharing communities

For many young people, their use of social networking websites, such as Facebook, is bound up with their social life, and most will want a degree of privacy in how they use these. Building a relationship with young people through doing digital life story work will often include discussion about how social networking websites are used. It is important to talk about the digital life story work material you create and what, if anything, can be more widely shared. As mentioned earlier in this book, Eileen Fursland's guide, *Social Networking and Contact* (2010) is a good general source to help you to consider how digital life story work relates to social networking websites.

The key way to assist responsible and safer internet use among young people is to talk to them. As working together is a key part of the digital life story work process, many issues concerning social networking and uploading content will be easier to discuss.

Key points to talk to young people about may include those listed below.

- The creative and exciting processes that went into making a film (copying, editing and re-using footage) can be used by others to alter the footage once the film is available online.

- Film can accidentally include information about the creator's location and personal details; we may not notice things that are very familiar to us and which could be used to identify us on our own film footage. If the young person you are working with is thinking about uploading a film to a website like YouTube, it is best to make the film specifically for the website, taking into account the use of neutral backgrounds and non-identifying information.

Blogs

A blog is a personal webpage upon which a user can write or present text, pictures and film clips. Blogs can take the form of diary entries, or might be about specific activities in a person's life or their thoughts on a subject that interests them. It is very easy to create blogs on the internet with the help of websites such as Blogger, and many blog creation websites, such as Piczo, are targeted specifically at teenagers. These sites offer templates which make creating a blog a simple process and require users to register on the site.

Photos and items like scrapbooks can be posted onto blogs with tools available through websites like Smilebox. All of the projects suggested in Chapter 2 could potentially be incorporated into a blog page; however, if a young person wants to start a blog, it is advisable to negotiate some ground rules about what sort of personal information they could include. It may help them to write about a specific theme or a topic they are interested in.

If you are unsure about the implications of blogging and internet safety, there is plenty of guidance available – some of it developed by schools or colleges that have used blogging in the classroom. Working together with the young person to look at suggested rules will help you negotiate their expectations. A few starting suggestions are given below.

- Do not use full names and addresses and other contact details such as email and phone numbers.

- Do not indicate future plans or activities that will reveal details of where you will be on specific days.

- If putting photos or film on the blog, make sure the people in the images are happy for you to do this.

- If giving an opinion on something or someone, make sure it is not unpleasant or upsetting to anyone – and remember, your opinion could be visible for some time. Do not disrespect people, groups of people or organisations.

- Information on the internet can remain there for a long time and be shared by others, so it can be very difficult to delete comments – remember that your blog, through its position on the internet, is essentially a public place.

Family history websites

Family history websites are not notably popular amongst young people compared with social networking websites. However, they are part of many tools and websites that people use to present themselves to the world. Registering on a family history/genealogy website can allow you to create quite complex family trees, with some allowing users to upload photos to attach to these.

Some websites can also search through public records offices and help the user to find people who could otherwise be hard to reach. Using such websites with the young person depends upon your relationship with them and their individual circumstances. Trying to represent complex family connections on these sites can be difficult, but this challenge is yet another way of discussing specific circumstances, family connections and structure. The material you upload to family history websites is usually private; however, many websites include options for inviting other people to contribute to family details and it is important that you look over these before engaging with young people in this way.

Looking back and moving on

We have suggested saving the digital life story material you have created with the young person in a designated folder on a computer. This is fine for most people – for the moment. Technology moves on rapidly and it is much easier to access information from a 20-year-old book than a 20-year-old digital device. Early storage devices included discs to insert into computers, which had a tiny storage capacity compared to today's DVDs. However, it is easy to see that DVDs and computer hard discs will change over time. It is therefore worthwhile to consider backing up the material in various formats. As computers and their memory capacity change, material can be re-worked and re-saved.

Some elements of digital life story work material will be created to enable the young person to grow in maturity, and some material will be "left behind" as the conversations around its creation or the work become forgotten. Of course, the materials are not finished products or simply evidence of such work being undertaken, but are the vehicle for conversations around the young person's life experiences, current circumstances and future aspirations. As young people move onto other avenues for expression and communication, the partnership created through working together on digital life story work can be continued.

As we change and mature, we reflect and transform how we see things in our lives. It can be useful to revisit material that was created early in the digital life story work process to provide an opportunity to discuss with the young person how things have changed and how new perspectives have formed. This can illustrate new emotions, complexity and contradictions, which might not have been so easy to see when you were involved in the projects.

Future directions for digital life story work

This book represents the culmination of a four-year research project undertaken at the Centre for Research on Children and Families in the University of East Anglia, in partnership with Norfolk County Council, BREAK and latterly with the assistance of Hertfordshire County Council. Many of the ideas were formed during the lead author's employment as a residential worker, involved in trying to fill a resource gap in interesting ways of communicating with adolescents about their past, present and future aspirations. This book, like many of the ideas contained within it, is a starting point. As the importance of digital technologies continues to grow in society, the need to embrace and use these same technologies positively with vulnerable populations will grow with it. To echo the comments of one residential home manager, 'We've got to get used to this sort of technology; it isn't going away'.

Following on from the four-year project research, Dr Simon P Hammond is in the initial stages of exploring the possibilities of undertaking a larger evaluative trial, which would aim to evaluate the usefulness of a bespoke, private blog called Memorify, as an approach to digital life story work. Conversations are ongoing at the time this book goes to print. Hopefully, this innovative resource will have the potential to be both a sustainable and an established part of practice when seeking to engage adolescents in life story work.

Useful references and further reading

Many of the ideas contained within this book were created by frontline practice experiences; others have been shaped by resources mentioned earlier. The list below represents a mixture of academic and non-academic texts cited in this book, with other publications deemed interesting also included.

Baynes P (2008) 'Untold stories: a discussion of life story work', *Adoption & Fostering*, 32:2, pp. 43–49

Dixon J (2007) 'Young people leaving residential care: experiences and outcomes', in Kendrick A (ed), *Residential Child Care: Prospects and challenges*, London: Jessica Kingsley Publishers, pp. 35–53

Fahlberg V (1994) *A Child's Journey through Placement*, London: BAAF

Fursland E (2010) *Social Networking and Contact*, London: BAAF

Fursland E (2011) *Social Networking and You,* London: BAAF

Gilligan R (2009) *Promoting Resilience* (2nd edn), London: BAAF

Hammond SP (2009) 'Updating life story work for use with a technologically proficient generation: a review', *Good Enough Caring Journal*, December, www.goodenoughcaring.com

Hammond SP (2011) 'Facebook friend or Facebook foe?', *Good Enough Caring Journal*, June, www.goodenoughcaring.com

Kendrick A (2005) 'Social exclusion and social inclusion: themes and issues in residential child care', in Crimmens MD (ed), *Facing Forward: Residential child care in the 21st century,* Lyme Regis: Russell House Publishing, pp. 7–18

Kendrick A (2008) *Residential Child Care: Prospects and challenges*, London: Jessica Kingsley Publishers

Lenhart A and Madden M (2007) 'Teens, privacy and online social networks', accessed 27 January 2010, www.pewinternet.org

Luckock B and Lefevre M (eds) (2008) *Direct Work: Social work with children and young people in care*, London: BAAF

Neil E, Cossar J, Jones C, Lorgelly P and Young J (2010) *Supporting Direct Contact after Adoption*, London: BAAF

Rees J (2009) *Life Storybooks for Adopted Children: A family friendly approach*, London: Jessica Kingsley Publishers

Rose R and Philpot T (2005) *The Child's Own Story: Life story work with traumatised children,* London: Jessica Kingsley Publishers

Ryan T and Walker R (2007) *Life Story Work* (3rd edn), London: BAAF

Schofield G and Beek M (2006) *Attachment Handbook for Foster Care and Adoption,* London: BAAF

Shah S and Argent H (2006) *Life Story Work: What is it and what it means,* London: BAAF

Stein M and Munro ER (2008) *Young People's Transitions from Care to Adulthood: International research and practice*, London: Jessica Kingsley Publishers

Steinfield C, Ellison NB and Lampe C (2008) 'Social capital, self-esteem, and use of online social network sites: a longitudinal analysis', *Journal of Applied Developmental Psychology,* 29:31, pp. 434–445

Taylor S (2010) *Narratives of Identity and Place,* London: Routledge

Thacker R and Hunter MA (2010) 'Empowering youth: use of technology in advocacy to affect social change', *Journal of Computer-Mediated Communication,* 15:4, pp. 575–591

Tregeagle S and Darcy M (2008) 'Child welfare and information and communication technology: today's challenge', *British Journal of Social Work,* 28, pp. 1481–1498

UNICEF (2002) *Adolescence: A time that matters,* New York, NY: UNICEF

Young J and Neil E (2009) 'Contact after adoption', in Schofield G and Simmonds J (eds), *The Child Placement Handbook: Research, policy and practice,* London: BAAF, pp. 241–259

Appendix 1

Equipment for digital life story work: what to choose and how to use

In choosing equipment for digital life story work, various factors need to be taken into consideration. Pragmatically, it is important to address the issue of cost, both in terms of time and money. At this point it is also worth reinforcing that the product produced is a secondary consideration to the process of undertaking the work, and the relationship formed with the young person. This mirrors how the aesthetic appeal of traditional life story work books similarly plays second fiddle to the therapeutic benefits of undertaking the work and the supportive relationship experienced. However, the digital elements of this approach do allow for polished products to be produced fairly efficiently (practical tips are offered at various points throughout this book). The equipment outlined here includes digital technologies used to record created material but also equipment used to store this material digitally.

Camcorders (estimated cost £150–£450)

Uses: Camcorders are very flexible handheld recording tools, meaning that the user is able to orientate the device in all directions. The majority of such devices are tapeless and rely upon a range of internal storage solutions. Many feature an LCD screen to allow users to view footage recorded and automatic recording modes designed to make filming easier.

Pros: LCD screens allow users to instantly review what they have recorded; the majority are tripod-compatible to make filming less shaky and have large storage capacities.

Cons: Advanced camcorders can cost anywhere up to £1,000, but such a high specification of equipment is not needed here. The high cost of such devices may make young people reluctant to use them for fear of breaking them. When using advanced features, batteries can quickly run flat.

Pocket camcorders (estimated cost £30–£200)

Uses: These are lightweight and compact alternatives to conventional camcorders. Designed to be more user-friendly, they can also be used more creatively when in motion as fear of breakage is lessened.

Pros: Lightweight, cheap(ish) and user-friendly, many require much less technological know-how as they are designed to "plug and play".

Cons: Dependent upon price, some pocket camcorders may lack the ability to zoom and require the additional purchase of batteries. Cheaper models may have a low amount of inbuilt storage and require additional memory cards.

Cameraphones and smartphones (estimated cost £50–£400)

Uses: Although not as advanced as purpose-built digital cameras/camcorders, they are likely to capture more spontaneous images and videos since their primary function (i.e. mobile phone) dictates that they are usually kept with users at all times. As they are mobile and compact, different types of recordings are possible.

Pros: Many young people own mobile phones with inbuilt cameras and are proficient in using them. Some mobiles also have inbuilt editing software. Phones are convenient, easily accessed, more mobile and commonly much more familiar to young people.

Cons: Lower image and video quality means that when content is displayed on larger screens (e.g. computers or TVs), pixelation may occur. Films may be jerky if the phone is handheld. Phones may have limited memory, so only short films can be taken.

Built-in webcams (no cost)

Uses: Can be used to record video diaries that can bypass any writing or literacy issues, supporting young people's ability to express emotions in their own words. Can also be integrated into digital media such as Skype and FaceTime (free internet-based calling programmes).

Pros: Cheap, as cost is included in the cost of overall computer/laptop/tablet.

Cons: Not as easy to orientate as removable webcams since many are inbuilt in the computer/laptop/tablet screen. Often lower quality sound and picture resolution.

Removable webcams (estimated cost £10–£35)

Uses: As with built-in webcams, they record audio and visual material and can be integrated into digital media such as Skype and FaceTime.

Pros: Can be orientated in any direction and removed where appropriate. Cheap and easy to install with many being "plug and play" devices. They record sound alongside video without the need for an additional microphone or headphones, and many can also double up as fixed digital cameras.

Cons: Dependent on cost, many can have fairly low image and video resolutions. Because they are removable, they can become lost and/or broken more readily than built-in webcams.

Appendix 2
Jargon buster

This appendix is not a comprehensive list of technological jargon, but introduces common phrases and terms used throughout the book. If in doubt, search for the term online in a search engine such as Google, or ask the young person.

Table 1: Common terms used in relation to taking pictures with digital cameras/camcorders

Term	What does this mean?
Pixel(s)	A term given to the smallest components of a picture or image displayed on a computer screen, these are the small single-coloured squares which make up the picture. Normally, the higher the number of pixels in an image, the higher the image quality.
Megapixel (MP or Mpx)	One million pixels. When buying a digital camera or device which includes a digital camera, the term megapixel (MP) is used by manufacturers to convey the quality of the image that the camera is capable of recording. Normally, the higher the number, the higher the quality of the picture will be. Some would argue that the difference between a 3MP and 4MP is negligible, but the difference between a 4MP and 20MP is obviously more profound.
HD (High Definition)	Like megapixels, HD or High Definition relates to image quality. For example, HDTV will display a picture in finer details, sharper colour and an overall better picture quality because it displays more pixels. HD camcorders do the same: they record a more detailed image even when the camcorder operator zooms in.
Pixelation	A term used to describe the picture distortion which occurs when the individual pixels which make up pictures become visible. Picture quality is particularly important when seeking to enlarge a picture onto a bigger scale. If the camera used to take the picture was 1MP rather than 4MP, there is a good chance that the picture would become quickly distorted if enlarged.

A general rule of thumb is that the higher the quality of a picture or video, the more complex the digital file it creates. As digital files become more complex, the file size increases, meaning that the amount of digital storage needed to store the file also increases. When storing digital files, certain terminologies are commonly used to describe file size and therefore the amount of memory required to store them. Table 2 introduces these terminologies and also describes different digital storage devices.

Table 2: Common terms used in relation to storing digital information

Term	What does this mean?
Byte	The smallest unit used to describe the storage of digital information.
Kilobyte (KB)	The unit used to describe 100,000 (10^3) bytes. For smaller and less complex files, KBs are commonly presented alongside the number of bytes. When creating simple text-based documents, KB will usually be the denomination used.
Megabyte(s) or "meg" (MB)	The unit used to describe 1,000,000 (10^6) bytes. When creating short video clips, MB will usually be the denomination used. Checking file size is important when looking to transfer video files and pictures.
Gigabyte(s) or "gig" (GB)	The unit used to describe 1,000,000,000 (10^9) bytes. When talking about digital storage devices for personal use, this is the most common denomination used. For example, electronic music devices now come with anywhere from 4GB–64GB of storage included. There are approximately 1024MBs to 1GB.
USB (Universal Serial Bus) socket	Rectangular sockets most commonly found on the front, back or side of a computer which allow the connection of a variety of devices. Much like an everyday plug socket, they were introduced to standardise how devices can be connected to computers.
USB/memory stick/pen/flash drive	Known by a variety of names, these devices replaced floppy disks and are frequently used to transfer digital data in a variety of formats from one computer to another. They are inserted into the computer's USB socket and can range in storage capacity from 4GB–512GB. The cost of such devices increases in line with storage capacity.
Secure Digital (SD) memory card	These cards are frequently used in a range of cameras and camcorders to store data, with this data transferred to computers via SD/miniSD/microSD drives on computers or USB-based card readers. There are a variety of SD cards available to purchase, and the names of these relate to the physical size of the cards (SDs are the largest, miniSDs second largest and microSDs the smallest). In contrast to USB memory sticks, some SD cards are read-only, and most feature protection tabs (similar to those of cassette tapes) which means data cannot be overwritten unless the tab is unlocked. Additionally, some password protected cards are available.
USB-based card readers	These devices are inserted into a computer's USB socket and allow the fast transfer of the content on SD cards onto the computer. Like the cards themselves, there are a wide variety of card readers available so be sure to purchase the one which works with your SD card type. Alternatively, there are card readers available which will work with all popular SD card types, but these tend to be more expensive.

Burning data to CDs or DVDs	This involves transferring/copying digital data files. This can only be done when the computer being used has a CD or DVD rewriter (see Chapter 6). This is a useful way of storing and archiving digital files.
DVD-R	A recordable DVD format. Data uploaded to this type of DVD cannot be changed. DVD-R is the oldest type of DVD format and recognisable in older DVD players. You can experiment with different DVD types with the DVD player to be used to watch the DVD.
DVD-RW/DVD-RAM/ DVD+R	A recordable DVD which is rewritable, in that data can be copied and deleted as the user desires. You can experiment with different DVD types with the DVD player to be used to watch the DVD.

Because this book encourages you to use a range of media files (pictures and video clips) and move these from the digital devices, which created them, onto computers, it is important to outline commonly used terms when transferring such files. Table 3 does this and introduces terms used when converting file types to those most appropriate for the software used on your computer.

Table 3: Common terms used when handling and transferring digital files

Term	What does this mean?
File extensions/file types	Digital technologies create a range of different file types. Common types include .pdf and .doc. These inform the computer what programme should be used to open the file or document (in this example, Adobe Reader and Word respectively).
File convertors	When using digital devices that record pictures and film clips, similar rules apply to those detailed above. Files are created with particular extensions; on occasion, it may be necessary to convert/change the file extension to allow the file to play on your computer's video or media player. There are a number of free online file converters. www.zamzar.com is one of the most popular and easy to use.
Media player	Software that plays a range of audio and audiovisual files (also known as multimedia files). The most common media players are Windows Media Player for PCs and QuickTime and iTunes for Mac.
.wmv, .avi, .mpeg, .mp4, .3gpp, .3gp, .mov	These abbreviations are common types of movie file. Before purchasing or filming with the various digital technologies, it is worth exploring what file types your computer supports easily and trying to match these to the equipment purchased. If the file type produced does not match your computer, the editing programmes which come with the equipment should allow you to create the file in the extension which is supported by your media player (check in devices/software instruction books). Additionally, depending on the size of the file, you may wish to use the online and free file convertors previously mentioned. This can appear daunting to new users, but this is why we recommend experimenting before beginning a project with the young person.
.mp3, .wma, .m4a	These abbreviations are the most common audio/music file types created by a range of technologies.

.jpeg, .jpg, .bmp	These abbreviations are common types of picture file. Unlike audio and movie files, these file types can be opened on both PC and Mac computers.

Having created content, the next step is to edit it. Table 4 introduces some common terms associated with editing digital material.

Table 4: Common terms used when editing digital pictures and movie files

Term	What does this mean?
Crop	A term used to describe the removal of the outer parts of an image. This function is common in most photo editing software and is a quick and simple way to resize an image or photo and get rid of unwanted background.
Trimming	Another word for editing. Trimming allows you to remove pieces at the beginning or end of the film clip to make it shorter. Trimming a clip allows you to use just the best part of a clip in your movie.
Storyboard view	Moviemaking software which features a storyboard view allows the user to arrange and rearrange contents easily, with each segment (either clip or picture) represented as a single box in a storyboard. In some moviemaking software, this view also allows you to add video effects and transitions easily.
Timeline view	Not all moviemaking software will feature a storyboard view but most, if not all, will feature some form of timeline view, which allows the user to see a more detailed view of the movie project they are creating. Timeline view can be used to review or modify the timing of the clips in your project, with some software allowing users to zoom in or out on particular details, whilst also allowing them to adjust audio levels and add more cinematic effects such as titles, credits and transitions.

Appendix 3
Cyberbullying resources

Below are a selection of websites of a range of independent and Government-funded resources created to combat the problem of cyberbullying. This is not a comprehensive list and a quick search of the internet should generate numerous helpful results. The resources and guidance provided by this appendix are designed to act as a starting point and point of reference.

www.stopcyberbullying.org/index2.html
A website run by Parry and the WiredKids Inc which features a host of practical and helpful tips written from a parent's perspective. It includes helpful sections on tackling the problem of cyberbullying and ways to prevent it.

www.bullying.co.uk/advice/young-people-advice/cyberbullying
Run by BullyingUK, this website has sections aimed at young people, schools and parents. In the young persons' section, there are a number of comprehensive guides and advisory articles on preventing and stopping cyberbullying. The parents' section includes a range of helpful case study articles written from the parent's perspective and also the option to join a discussion forum.

It is also worth looking at examples from UK-based children's charities such as:

- **ChildLine www.childline.org.uk/Explore/Bullying/Pages/CyberBullying.aspx**
- **NSPCC www.nspcc.org.uk**
- **Kidscape www.kidscape.org.uk/cyberbullying**

All offer comprehensive information and advice on cyberbullying from various perspectives and frequently update their resources and advice.

Appendix 4
Filming and editing tips

Remove the lens cap

Obvious and avoidable, but probably something everyone has failed to do at one point.

Holding the camcorder

Ideally, encourage people to hold the camcorder in front of them. This gives the built-in microphone the optimum chance of recording the young person's voice, and also allows the camera operator to walk around holding the camcorder safely. Occasionally, when young people are enthusiastically telling stories, they may bring the camcorder down by their side, as it can feel quite strange telling a story whilst holding the camcorder upright. Balance the desire to create aesthetically pleasing content with not interrupting young people's stories while they are in mid-flow.

Rotating the camcorder

There is nothing more frustrating than trying to watch a series of clips with your head turned to the side. Unlike pictures, films are not easy to rotate when editing. Encourage young people to record footage holding the camcorder properly to avoid neck-ache and frustrating content.

Impact of weather

The weather in the UK can be grey, windy and rainy at times. When planning filming, think about how this can affect how memories will be represented on film. Film clips that are dark and grey, despite the positive stories shared, can sometimes come across as sad.

Zooming

Camcorders with a zoom function are helpful. However, constantly being zoomed in makes devices hard to keep steady and results in jerky sections of film. Being overly zoomed in can also make films look pixelated, particularly if they are recorded in low definition. Tripods can help but for podwalking purposes, they are cumbersome to carry around.

Filming from inside or outside the car

For the podwalking project, a crucial part of this approach is the actual business of walking around in the places visited, rather than viewing them from inside a car. Walking around places is a much "freer" process than filming from a car, and also slower. By spending more time in places, stories can emerge slowly as opposed to being rushed or prematurely ended by a car pulling away. Undertaking a podwalk from within a car does allow for more ground to be covered and a greater range of stories to be told. However, projects need to be based upon the therapeutic quality of stories and the process itself rather than simply the quantity of stories shared. It is also much harder for the facilitator to be attentive and respond in a supportive manner if they are driving.

Useful web resources on film-making

www.ehow.com/ehow_tech-video-and-camcorders/
This website provides a range of up-to-date practical instructions, advice and articles on how to get the best from a range of digital devices.

www.wikihow.com/Use-a-Camcorder
This wiki (a website developed by a community of individuals which allows any user to add and edit content) features a step-by-step guide, numerous tips and links to other useful sites. As it is a wiki, it has the added benefit of being written in a more accessible style and more readily updated.

www.youtube.com
Do not underestimate how helpful YouTube can be in providing video tutorials and a host of helpful tips specific to your model of camcorder. Of the many videos on the website, those provided by the New York Video School – www.nyvs. com – are among the best.

Editing and producing DVDs

There are already many simple video tutorials available on the internet for popular video editing and DVD-making software. These can be found by entering search terms such as "How to edit a movie file in..." They are particularly useful as they allow you to go at your own pace and replay elements you might have missed or not understood. The following hyperlinks were particularly useful during the original research project on which this book is based and should be used as a starting point.

www.youtube.com/watch?v=HygFZq5mW1s
As frequently mentioned in this book, video-sharing platforms such as YouTube provide an endless supply of tutorials created by amateur subscribers. This short clip demonstrates how to add captions in Windows Live Movie Maker.

www.which.co.uk/technology/archive/guides/beginners-guide-to-video-editing/
This link provides a beginner's guide to video editing, organised in a simple step-by-step format. It covers many aspects, from importing content to burning it to a DVD.

http://windows.microsoft.com/en-GB/windows-live/movie-maker-get-started
or
www.apple.com/findouthow/movies
These links provides a starting point for how to import photos and videos, edit your movies and audio and produce DVDs for both Microsoft and Mac computers.

These final links are a starting point for how to print your own CD or DVD labels and covers.

www.online-tech-tips.com/computer-tips/free-cd-label-maker-software/

www.pcworld.com/article/210178/how_to_print_labels.html

www.ehow.com/video_4871927_create-dvd-labels.html

www.wikihow.com/Make-a-DVD-Cover

www.ehow.com/how_5069882_make-cover-using-microsoft-word.html

Appendix 5
Worksheet for use with the young person

This worksheet can be used with the young person with whom you will be undertaking digital life story work. By discussing their answers with them, you can explore their expectations of the work and negotiate ground rules for the project.

What do I expect?

What do I expect from the person helping me with the project?

What do I want to get from this project?

Which bits of the project do I expect to be boring?

Are there any parts of the project which I'm worried/confused about?

Which parts of the project do I expect to become frustrated with?

Which bits of the project do I expect to be fun?